Best CEOs

Best CEOs

How The Wild, Wild Web Was Won

Ian Halperin

Ogo Books

This title is available at special quantity discounts for bulk
purchases for sales promotions, premiums, fund raising, educational or
institutional use. For details, contact: sales@ogobooks.com, or write to:
Ogo Books, P.O. Box 23140, Ottawa, Ontario, Canada K2A 4E2.

Visit our Web site at www.ogobooks.com

First printing 2001

10 9 8 7 6 5 4 3 2 1

Printed in Canada

The key to a job is to get rewarded! This book is dedicated to the those dot-com entrepreneurs who worked so hard for so long but never became rich. Many went out of business. I hope that by reading the success stories in this book they'll be inspired to start-up again!

About The Author

Award-winning author Ian Halperin has contributed articles about the high-tech scene to numerous publications across North America.   He is the author of five highly acclaimed books and has worked for the Montreal Gazette, BBC, Toronto Globe & Mail and the CBC's Fifth Estate. Recently, Halperin has been written about in the New York Times, Boston Globe, Toronto Star, Time magazine, and the New Yorker; he's also appeared on NBC, VH-1, ABC, Court TV, TSN and Global TV.

Halperin is popular on the North American lecture circuit, giving motivational speeches about how to power schmooze and succeed in the high-tech industry.

For additional:

- blue bags
- delivery boxes
- delivery labels

please email:

deliveryhub @tpl.toronto.on.ca

03032 HBS

Contents

Motivational Quotes to inspire you from some "Non-Techs"

Spend enough time around success and failure, and you learn a reverence for possibility
- *Dale Daulton*, syndicated business columnist

It is hard to fail, but it is worse never to have tried to succeed - *Theodore Roosevelt*

I don't know the key to success, but the key to failure is trying to please everybody - *Bill Cosby*

The ability to concentrate and to use your time well is everything - *Lee Iacocca*

Freedom lies in being bold - *Robert Frost*

Success is 99 percent failure - *Soichiro Honda*

If you can dream it, you can do it - *Walt Disney*

I could use a hundred people who don't know there is such a word as impossible - *Henry Ford*

Acknowledgments

I am deeply indebted to a number of people for their cheerful and dedicated help during the two years it took to research and write this book. First among these is Esmond Choueke, my friend and colleague, who worked with me as closely as anyone possibly could. Kevin Sheehan provided excellent direction and helped put the whole project together. I thank my researchers for their tenacious efforts to find elusive people and persuade them to be interviewed. Todd Shapiro helped with good humor and insight. And most of all I would like to thank Jennifer Walker for valuable insight and direction. Without her this project could not have got off the ground.

I'm also indebted to many sources for background information, including Business 2.0, Forbes Magazine, The Standard.com, Business Week, The Wall Street Journal, The New Yorker, Worth , Silicon Valley North, Moneyline, Time, The Washington Post and Newsweek.

I also want to thank and acknowledge the contributions of: Alvin Hill, Fred Barnett, Jill Higgins, John MacKey, Bob Bailey, Steven Garcia, Larry King, Elroy Jones, Chaim Segal, Jane Stevenson, Paul Devine, Julien Feldman, Daniel Sanger, Santo Tadeo, Lou Greene, Dorie Simmonds, Renata Butera, Josh Tyler, Richard Gold, Fred Reed, Delano Juridini, Joanne Jones, Stuart Nulman, Nick Chursinoff, Jean Pierre Ouissett, Bruce Pascal, Helen Hefter, Sticky Reisler, Mark Fleming, Jaime Roskies, Kristian Kostov, Pierre Turgeon, Mario Tuchi, The New York Subway, The LA Freeway, James Grant, Lori Gordon, Andrea Bradley, Antonio Morchina, Jarvis Plante, Al "Media Circus" Sutherland, Jacquie Charleton, Gerry Wagschal, Chapters Book Buddies, Samantha Banton, Michael "Off The Record" Landsberg, Humble and Fred, Arlene Bynon, Johnnie

Oakley, Bruce Ward, Tadashi Onitsuka, Warren Lee, Warren Tannenbaum, Bobby White, Matt Radz, Jacob Horowitz, Tom Grant, Stephen Sanderson, Mike Friedleib, Jermaine Stewart, Allan Young, The Chodats, Marcy Bonavista, Kenneth Smythe, Michel Brown, Troy Hartman, George "Guido" Bartucci, Wayne Rogers, Mandy Bryden, Chaney Allen, Danielle Redding, Patrick Glemaud, Juluis Grey, Don Cosenza, Terry Adams, Margaret Henry, Dr. Ron Gottlieb, George Nesbitt, Liz Cargo, Robert Choueke, Bert Rubinstein, Lisa Hull, Jordan Singerman, Nichole McGill, Ken Heinrich, Tony Biscoe, Keith Bateman, Justin Wheeler and Jason Santini. Most of all, I would like to thank my entire family for their support and encouragement.

The Opening Bell

The Internet has grown at a much faster pace than the Industrial Revolution that began in the 18th century. E-commerce has become a major factor in the gross domestic product for the world. In 1999, information technology companies were responsible for more than one-third of the United States' economic growth. Out of a 5 percent improvement in U.S. production of goods and services in 1999, 1.6 percent is attributable to information technology, a Commerce Department report revealed. And the rest of the world has followed suit. In Germany and Japan e-commerce is becoming the most popular way of doing business. In the U.K. and France the most popular field that parents prefer their children to get an education is in high-tech.

"It used to be that parents encouraged their kids to become doctors and lawyers," says Debrah Sanders, a London based headhunter. "Most parents today tell their kids to study engineering or computer programming.

15

About 90 percent of the jobs I fill are in the computer industry."

From 1998-2000, the e-commerce workforce in the U.S. grew by more than 40 percent. to 3.2 million. And these workers are making average salaries of $58,000, almost double than all other private industry employees.

Best CEOs...How The Wild, Wild Web Was Won makes light of how the Internet's top moguls hustled their way into power, grabbed hold of the world's economy by storm, and made billion dollar fortunes just about by the click of a mouse. Over 150 people highly connected in the e-commerce industry were interviewed to break into the leading ranks of the fascinating CEOs who dared to sway from the "old" way of business and chanced the miraculous possibilities of doing business online. The objective: to create a most useful and compelling motivational book, **one that nobody on the Internet can afford to be without.**

By reading about the struggles and successes of Internet giants Timothy Koogle of Yahoo, Steve Jobs of Apple, Larry Ellison of Oracle or recent up-and-comers like Margaret Whitman, what you get is a no-nonsense book to launching and maintaining a business on the Internet, covering all points from sales and marketing to the very technical side of e-commerce. As Intuit founder Scott Cook says, "it isn't going to be easy, but with ambition, creativity, and access to the right information (i.e. this book), it's possible to do e-business with the best of them".

Best CEOs views of the digital future - from hardware to software to online services - is a must read for all who use technology in their business today or plan to use it on the road ahead. This motivational book charts the course successful e-businesses are following and shrewd business people would be wise to follow.

This remarkable new crop of billionaire achievers has turned the existing power structure inside out, shattering the old way of doing business that has united the world's commercial elite for so long. Their pursuit of money is not premeditated by the desire to own lots of fancy homes, cars and to ride in a private jet. "We don't have the ostentatious spending habits of millionaires of the past like Howard Hughes," said Jason Wright, a Silicon Valley native who owns several dot-com sites. "We're driven by the pursuit of advancing in a technologically sophisticated world. We're more interested in making history and having a big impact on the progress of the world. And if you do that successfully the money and prestige comes regardless."

The biggest challenge today facing business leaders is struggling to keep pace with the Net. Most of these leaders recognize the importance of the Internet and technology in their overall business strategy, but have been slow connecting their businesses online. According to a Business Week survey most CEOs' number one priority is developing customer relationships. Less than 25 percent said e-commerce is a major concern. This attitude has alarmed the world's leading business analysts.

"Most business leaders are not maximizing the large number of opportunities that e-commerce presents," says Johnathan Weinberg, the well-known Wall Street investment analyst. "In the short term it might make sense. But when the full impact of the e-commerce revolution sets in these people will be scrambling to get caught up. They'll lose big money because they were stubborn and slow to adapt to the new way."

Whether you want to an increased income, or to wake up everyday and feel good about your job, or to become a Best CEO yourself, this book tells you how. Who knows, you too could soon be surfing the net with the big boys!

Introduction -
The King Of Amazon

When people look back in 100 years on the history of the Internet and the important pioneers who developed it, the name Jeff Bezos will loom larger than most. The head of Amazon.com, Bezos is considered by many as being one of the most successful young CEOs ever. His motto is customer satisfaction comes first and foremost. Then, Bezos believes, the cash will automatically roll in. It's a system that makes Bezos extremely popular with his employees, whom he deals with closely on a personal level.

"He likes to be called by his first name and he wants people to look forward to going to work," says an Amazon.com manager. "It's his unorthodox way of doing business. And it works perfectly. His infectious smile and boyish humor rub off on the rest of the company, creating an incredible team oriented environment. Jeff makes sure that there's never a dull moment at Amazon. Working there is totally rewarding and fun."

Bezos grew up in New Mexico, Texas, and Florida spending summers on his grandparents' ranch in south Texas where his regular chores included windmill repair and cattle castration. He graduated from Princeton University with a degree in computer science. He spent four years analyzing stocks for a hedge fund and was inspired to start Amazon when he learned that the number of people using the Internet had grown by 2,300 percent in a single year. He quit his job and Amazon.com was born. "I knew that it was a once in a lifetime opportunity," Bezos says. "If I passed up the chance I would have regretted it when I was 80."

Bezos and his wife Mackenzie drove in a Chevy Blazer from Texas to Seattle, where Bezos launched his new venture. Today, Amazon has jettisoned from a books, music and video online vendor into the world's biggest shopping mall. Besides investing in HomeGrocer.com and Drugstore.com Bezos introduced "zShops" which permits anybody to rent space on Amazon to sell whatever they want.

In 1999 Bezos, only 35, became the fourth youngest person to be voted Time Magazine's Man Of The Year, preceded by Charles Lindbergh, 25, in 1927; Queen Elizabeth II, 26, in 1952; and Martin Luther King Jr., 34, in 1963. Time called Bezos "a pioneer, royalty and a revolutionary - noble for company for the man who is, unquestionably, king of cybercommerce. Jeff Bezos has done more than construct an online mall. He's helped build the foundation of our future."

Today, Bezos is worth more than $10 billion. Here's some advice from interviews with Mr. Bezos over the years that he offers to anybody interested in doing business on the Internet, and to potential future E-commerce CEOs:

"At Amazon.com what we're doing is making it easier for readers to connect with books and for publishers to connect with customers.

"The key to doing business on the Internet for any E-commerce outfit is that you have to recognize that the web today is a pain to use. It's a new technology. You have to figure out a way to offer credibly strong value proposition to your customers. People shop at Amazon.com because of strong selection and strong discounting policies combined with information about the books and the convenience of shipping them to your home or office desk. If you do something that can be offered from something of a more traditional method like a paper catalogue than you're not offering strong value proposition.

"One of our customers is a famous guy named Bill Gates who said he shops at Amazon.com because we have a big selection, it's convenient and we're reliable. I think he touched every reason for shopping online with us

except for one, that we're the broadest discounters in the world.

"With the traditional commerce way too much energy goes into marketing mediocre products and services. With E-commerce a big problem is the logistics and the customer service - the nonglamorous parts of the business. A lot of these companies that are coming online spend all their money and effort building a beautiful Web site and then can't get the stuff to the customers. It's important that the customer comes first. Word of mouth will make or break you. That's how we gauge how good a job we are doing.

"If we do a good job satisfying our customer over the Internet word of mouth is a hundred more times powerful than in the real world.

"We're just at the beginning of the Internet. The Internet today is like the Big Bang. A huge amount has happened and a huge amount is going to come."

- Jeff Bezos,
CEO Amazon.com

1

John Chambers

Your first impression of John Chambers is of someone who is busy-busy, one of the workers getting on with the job. Most big CEOs are rarely seen around their company's headquarters. They're too busy mingling with the "important" folks. Not one John Chambers. He's on a first name basis with just about everybody at Cisco. And his office door is usually open for employees to come in and sound off. He encourages his workers to voice their opinions. And it seems today that just about everyone has an opinion about John Chambers's personality, lifestyle, business tactics, products, motives, - and how he should be handling his immense fortune.

Some say that the projects he is financing are too big or too risky. Or they say he's only doing it to expand Cisco Systems's markets, or, especially, to keep boosting his public image in light of the heavy media attention he received in early 2000, when he temporarily took over the crown as the world's richest CEO from Bill Gates and Larry Ellison.

"I don't think many people envy John Chambers's situation," says New York Internet financial analyst Andrew Rhodes. "He came in from left field and suddenly became the world's most powerful CEO. Although Bill Gates has had his problems he has a lot of supporters and has become a cultural icon in the U.S. and around the world. He's the butt of so many jokes. Now everybody has to shift focus to John Chambers, a man who likes to do things behind the scenes and isn't nearly as flamboyant as a Bill Gates. It's the same type of thing when George Bush replaced Ronald Reagan as

President...Bush was boring and didn't have the charisma of Reagan. The media and public were lulled to sleep."

John Chambers does not fit the stereotypical bill of other successful Internet CEOs, of starting a small home business from nothing and struggling to make it work. Many of the Internet's top moguls started out with a computer in their garage, like Amazon.com's Jeff Bezos. Chambers didn't start Cisco Systems and never worked with its founders. He was not a computer nerd like many other successful CEOs. In fact, it was only a few years ago that Chambers didn't even know how to turn on a computer. A lawyer and an MBA, Chambers does not have a technical clue about the products his company sells. So how did the secretive, sensitive and shy Chambers become the top CEO in the world?

"He works, lives and loves according to his own set of rules," says former Cisco associate John Magedon. And nobody questions what he does. His motto to his employees is you do the technical stuff and leave the business to me. And it works like magic."

Chambers, the son of two medical doctors from Charleston, West Virginia, likes to keep his office open and accessible to his fellow workers. In fact, there is nothing ostentatious about his surroundings and one would not think that he was one of the world's wealthiest CEOs when visiting his office. The only window looks into a hallway and aside from a few family pictures there is nothing that Chambers proudly displays to impress visitors. "John's a very simple man who does not look down at his employees," said one Cisco employee. "He's the perfect example of how a CEO should act in today's world. That's why when you look around the faces don't change much. I've had offers to work elsewhere for more money but as long as John's at Cisco that's where I'll be. John makes us feel like one big family."

Chambers rarely speculates on the impulses and motives that motivate his corporate maneuvers. As Cisco continues to grow rapidly and dominate its markets a decade after going public, it has managed to create the highest capitalization of any company in the world next to Microsoft. "If not for Chambers this would have never

28

happened," Magedon says. "It was a perfect marriage. Why aren't other Internet companies as successful as Cisco? Simple, because you have technicians trying to be businessmen. It doesn't work. You need someone with a business background like John Chambers calling the shots. Engineers don't go to school to learn how to make deals. Many Internet companies go bust because they didn't take care in hiring successful solid business people aside from the technical staff."

For all its clout on Wall Street, Cisco does not strike a chord with the general public like Yahoo or Microsoft. Many people have not even heard of the company. One of a plethora of companies started in the eighties out of the Department of Computer Science at Stanford University, Cisco manufactures hardware and software that are rarely used by the home PC user. Its products are the world's most sophisticated for global data networks. And global is the key word. Cisco is bigger in Japan than in the U.S., a unique scenario for that restrictive nation.

"Japan is very competitive and its almost impossible to maintain a stranglehold on the market there," says Lydia Dorfman, a U.S. Internet strategist economic developer. "But Cisco is able to replace its products quickly as soon as they become obsolete, making it extremely difficult for anybody else to move in."

Chambers's strategy for growth is simple: whatever research and development its engineers cannot create in-house, it buys. That pays off in a variety of ways. A start-up company on the verge of releasing a new product, for example, will see it explode on the market - under the Cisco name. Cisco also uses acquisitions to gain talent for its entire organization. A case in point is Michelangelo Volpi, Cisco's vice-president of business development who has been the vital cog in pursuing acquisitions for Cisco. Before he came on the scene, Cisco had acquired a handful of companies. Since Volpi arrived in 1993, Cisco has acquired dozens of companies."

Companies

- ✗ Amazon
- ✗ Cisco
- ✗ Dell

"I believe that you're only as strong as the people you surround yourself with," Chambers said. "That not only applies to business but also to life. I'm fortunate that I've been able to have excellent support and expertise from the people who work at Cisco. It makes my job all that much easier and creates an environment of quality productivity. Under those circumstances you don't have to look back. It's full steam ahead."

Chambers's most important asset is his ability to grow the business rapidly and avoid mistakes that could prove costly. Before Chambers arrived at Cisco in 1991 from previous sales jobs at Wang and IBM, Cisco had paved the way for the commercialization of the Internet by building most of the routers that carry the global network's digital signals. Chambers transformed Cisco into a switch company, then as an end-to-end digital service company, and presently as a data/voice/video network company, competing with and staying ahead of stalwarts Nortel Networks and Lucent Technologies.

"Chambers is a master of calculating bigger markets and new opportunities," says Internet investment analyst Larry Gobeil. "The reason why he's so successful is that he doesn't rest on his past laurels. He pushes ahead, briskly and carefully. He's probably the smartest person to ever run an Internet company. Before he arrived at Cisco they were having lots of problems and were in much need of new structures and financing. John Chambers quickly addressed the companies needs and they've never had to look back."

When Chambers does err he is known to recover more quickly than anyone else. For example, in the beginning of 1999 he said he wanted the traditional telephone on his desk to be gone in 12 months. "In one year I won't need this anymore if everything goes as planned," he told the media. A year later in March 2000 his old phone was still there. Chambers immediately returned to the drawing board and used a backup plan. He unveiled plans for an office telephone system based on Internet technology. The new concept would transmit voice calls in the electronic language of the Internet and would undoubtedly push Cisco to the top of the burgeoning Internet-telephone market.

Experts predicted that Cisco would push past Nortel and Lucent Technologies, who are also developing Internet phone systems for offices. Merrill Lynch immediately announced plans to make Cisco's the main phone system at a new campus in Hopewell, New Jersey, installing 5,000 phones in just over one year. Texas Instruments also jumped on board. Bigwigs from both companies raved publicly about Cisco's latest product.

"You can plug the phone into any connection, and it will keep the same number you had," said Brian J. Bonner, chief information officer and a vice president at Texas Instruments. "You can take your phone and plug it in at a TI office in Germany, for instance, and I can dial your number, which looks like Dallas, and it rings in Germany."

Once again, Chambers turned a possible failure into a gem. And he got more publicity than ever. The media around the world, including CNN, Time, and USA Today descended on Chambers and Cisco. "That's the secret of John Chambers's success," said Internet business mogul Lou Barton. "When everything seems

33

bleak and about to collapse he pulls something out of his hat at the eleventh hour."

While Chambers continues to turn whatever he touches into gold his competitors breathe down his back, trying to convince the media and public that Cisco does not have a long term strategic advantage. In a June 2000 interview with investment author Larry MacDonald, Nortel CEO John Roth lashed out at Cisco. "Cisco is a tremendously powerful marketing company," Roth said. "But they don't have the depth of understanding we have in optical networking. This is not a simple technology. I think Cisco underestimates the complexity of making these systems perform."

Roth's criticism was not taken too seriously by Chambers's close followers. "Like in any other business it's a case of the competition trying to make the other person look bad," said California Internet venture capitalist Stan Geddes. "I think John Roth was trying to deliver a message to Chambers in light of all of Cisco's recent success. Basically what he really was saying is that 'you might be on top now but watch out because the minute you make a mistake we'll be there to take over the lead.'"

In November 2000 Chambers once again had the last laugh. Cisco reported fiscal first-quarter profits of 18 cents a share, shattering the forecast of analysts surveyed by First Call/Thomson Financial by a penny. Sales rose 66 percent year-on-year, eclipsing Wall Street projections. Chambers left Nortel and Lucent grasping for air. At the time, Nortel was down 13 percent and Lucent was down a whopping 67 percent. Chambers and Cisco forecast an increase of 50 to 60 percent in 2001.

"I think that John Roth could still eventually come out ahead when it's all over with, but it's not going to be easy," said one Wall Street investment strategist. "As long as John Chambers is there it's going to be an uphill battle. It's impossible to predict what Chambers has up his sleeve. He seems to always do the impossible."

Meanwhile, Chambers and his large entourage of advisors continue to keep a close eye on the market and use their deep pockets - more than $4 billion in cash plus a huge vault of Cisco shares - to buy more companies in the flow of Internet changes.

2

Scott McNealy

Scott McNealy once had a lot in common with Bill Gates, or so Scott believed. In the early days of his career, Scott was shy, introverted and was considered to be a bit of a nerd by people in his close circles, a fair description of Gates as well. For years their career paths tracked one another closely. When Gates and Microsoft became the world's most powerful business, McNealy began to reinvent himself with the spirit of a street fighter.

McNealy became critical, crude, coy and, most of all, very outspoken. In fact, when a federal judge ruled on June 7, 2000 that Microsoft should be broken into two companies, McNealy was ecstatic. For years he campaigned hard against Gates and Microsoft, desperately trying to get the balance of power in the technology industry tilted. In March 1998, McNealy told a U.S. Senate committee that Microsoft should be held to a different standard because it is a monopoly given the presence of Microsoft operating systems on more than 85 percent of PCs. And he challenged Gates's contention that Microsoft had less dominance in the PC industry than IBM once had.

"There is on huge difference," McNealy said. When IBM dominated the industry, information technology played a far smaller role in the economy and in the lives of people than it does today," he said. "As Microsoft seeks to leverage its operating system and application monopolies up into the enterprise, down into consumer products, and into the Internet, it has the power to affect the economy and the way we live and work that IBM, even at its zenith, never had."

McNealy quickly became the enemy over at Microsoft headquarters in Redmond, Washington.

38

Microsoft vice president for developer relations Tod Nielsen plastered his office with 241 photographs of McNealy, along with the coffee-cup symbol that represents Sun's well-known Java software. Neilson focused in on eliminating this enemy. At the end of each day, if Nielsen felt he had done something to put a dent into Sun, he would perform a ritual exercise. He checked off one of the photos with a conquering air.

McNealy seized every possible opportunity he had in public and in the media to poke fun at Microsoft. When, for example, Microsoft challenged Sun to fork over its Java programming language to an industry standards body, McNealy shot back: "Having Microsoft give us advice on open standards is like W.C. Fields giving moral advice to the Mormon Tabernacle Choir."

It troubled McNealy that Microsoft had become such a powerful entity. He felt needed to balance things out. He called Microsoft's office "a 250-megabyte hairball". In a tongue-in-cheek fall lineup for MSNBC, he called Microsoft execs Steve Ballmer and Gates

"Ballmer & Butt-head". McNealy's sarcasm was gobbled up eagerly by the world's leading hi-tech jourmalists.

"Everyone knows that Scott wanted to bitch about Microsoft's dominance," says hi-tech scribe Joel Hewitt. "If he went about it in another way it would have definitely been looked at as being sour grapes. But because he used such funny one-liners the media took a liking to him and started printing everything he said. Between the lines they saw reality in what Scott was saying. And in the end it hurt both Gates and Microsoft. I'm not sure whether or not Scott was coached on this one, but it turned out to be a brilliant strategy. He always came out smelling like roses."

McNealy grew up in modest surroundings in suburban Detroit. His family instilled in him a hard work ethic. His father William was the vice chairman of the fledgling American Motors Corporation. AMC was a good business lesson for the young Scott. While AMC scrambled hard to muster sufficient market share, Scott became aware of how difficult it is to succeed in business without the financial, technological and marketing clout to shape the direction of the industry.

"I think that Scott's father's experience has always stayed with him," says journalist Tara White. "He learned about how hard it is to succeed and how easy it is to fail."

McNealy got his first job at age 17, washing cars for $1.75 an hour at a Chevrolet dealership in Southfield, Michigan. Ironically, the dealership was owned by another high achiever, Roger Penske, who years later achieved fame as America's number one Indianapolis 500 auto racing mogul. McNealy looked up to Penske and dreamt of one day succesful like him.

McNealy was eager to learn as much as possible about business. He read the business section of the newspapers religiously. He was on his way to becoming a top scholar and achiever. He studied hard and received an undergraduate degree in economics from Harvard and an MBA from Stanford. In 1982, McNealy founded Sun, originally an acronym for Stanford University Network, with fellow Stanford MBA Vinod Khosla, Stanford

41

engineering graduate student, Andreas Bechtolsheim and William Joy, a software developing genius from the University of California at Berkeley.

Sun started building computer work stations mainly for engineers and scientists using a software system called Unix, a programming language that was originally the brainchild of AT&T's Bell Labs. A few years later, Sun made headlines around the world when it set a new standard in computing by inviting the industry to clone its Sparc microprocessor and AT&T's Unix. McNealy was credited for developing the one-technology-fits-all vision, a chip standard and operating system that was able to span any home computer to the most sophisticated corporate machines.

McNealy yearned to get a piece of the desktop PC business, a project that inside Sun was known as "Sparcintosh", a computer that would combine a PC chip with Apple Macintosh's huge consumer following. But McNealy could not withstand the pressure by desktop stalwarts Hewlett-Packard and IBM. McNealy is determined to be the leader on the Internet, which he says represents the "third wave of computing," the first being the mainframe era and the personal computer the second.

"McNealy always has a backup plan. That's why he is so successful," says Internet guru Toby Hircho. "He knows that not everything he tries will turn to gold. That's why he always has his workers experimenting in other areas. And if his plan fails he works twice as hard at something else to bounce back. Nobody in the industry is capable of bouncing back the way he does."

Few people have lived a more eventful life over the past two decades or so than Scott McNealy. And few people have more desperately needed such a makeover to shake off a lingering weight of pious myths. One persistent story is about McNealy being cheap, despite owning almost 3 billion dollars worth of Sun shares. "When we used to go for lunch it would often be at a cheap fast food joint," recalled Eric Schmidt, who worked for years as Sun's chief technology officer before becoming a successful CEO himself at Novell. "The bill would usually be about ten bucks for two. Scott McNealy just hates wasting money, hates spending a lot for things."

The stories range from McNealy's fondness for inexpensive meals to rumors that he cuts his old clothing into rags and saves up old soap.

McNealy is a veritable icon of Silicon Valley. He simply exudes everything there is about the American Dream. The boyish-looking 45-year-old chairman of Sun, even from sanitized accounts by his friends, is an insatiable businessman who has barely reached his mature stride. "Everybody talks about what Scott's done but it's nothing compared to what he has up his sleeve for the future," says Alan Liteman, who knew McNealy in the early nineties. "In any era Scott would have been the major dominant business force he is today. He knows every trick in the book about running a big business. And he's not afraid of failure." Liteman hastens to point out that McNealy's lifestyle is not everything it might appear. "He doesn't care about fancy cars and big houses. He's more interested in posting good numbers for his company. Scott's the type of guy who could have 100 million dollars in his wallet and still dine out at Burger King."

At Sun's headquarters in Mountain View, California there are no traces of unnecessary spending. There are no indoor pools, no VIP spas or reserved spaces. Nobody is allowed to personalize the company stationary. "Scott does not spend a cent more than he has to," Liteman says. "That's his recipe for success and it has worked for him brilliantly for such a long time. I don't think he should be labeled as being cheap, just wise. Some CEOs spend thousands on corporate art for the walls and fancy company cars and drive their companies into serious debt because of their lavish lifestyles. Many go bankrupt. Scott's above all that crap."

In 1995, McNealy moved closer to achieving his goal of "providing connectivity to anyone, anywhere, anytime, on any device". Java technology became McNealy's biggest product ever. The media took close note. In July 1999, The Wall Street Journal praised Java for setting a new industry standard, saying "Java is fast emerging as a key tool for building new software applications that streamline business management and power Internet commerce."

While McNealy surges ahead and laughs his way to the bank as Sun remains a premier growth stock, showing 20 percent gains in revenue and profits in fiscal 1999, there remains a long line of detractors. "McNealy has a long history as a charlatan," said Internet columnist Jesse Berst. "For years he preached the mantra of "open computing" with Unix, while simultaneously building his own proprietary version. Then he mounted a campaign to force Microsoft to put Windows in the public domain. 'For the good of customers' he said sanctimoniously. For the good of Sun Microsystems was more like it."

McNealy isn't at all concerned about his competition and enemies. In fact, he says, they tend to keep him more on his toes. "In any business no matter how well you do your job you will be criticized," he says. "If you sit around all day feeling bad about it you won't get too far. You just got to go forwards, and continue doing the best job you can."

<u>3</u>

S*tephen* C*ase*

Dan Case couldn't believe what had happened on the eleventh day of the new millennium. It was supposed to be his big day. Dan, who heads Chase H&Q, was supposed to be the center of attention, hosting several thousand biotechnology executives, venture capitalists and money managers at a four-day conference in San Francisco. Finally, he would escape from living in the shadow of his younger brother Steve.

The media bombarded Dan with questions at the opening of the conference, but for all the wrong reasons. Once again Dan was upstaged and faced with questions about his whiz kid brother. Steve didn't intentionally plan it that way but his company America Online had just made a $184 billion offer to buy Time Warner. Steve masterminded the pending Time Warner merger. Dan sarcastically joked about it during a luncheon address that day: "That little deal in Virginia. I'll have to remember to thank them for the timing on that."

The Time Warner deal created a company with a combined market value of almost $350 billion. Soon after, Case announced his intention of relinquishing the CEO title when the merger completion is final. Many of his colleagues were caught off guard. "I guess he felt that he wouldn't be able to top that," said New York Internet financial analyst Mark Benson. "And I don't think you can blame him. This has got to be the biggest blockbuster merger ever. The man can walk away with his head up. He created history with this deal. It will be analyzed in classrooms and boardrooms for centuries."

During the next few months, as Time Warner became absorbed into America Online, many concerns arose about whether Time Inc. magazines will receive special treatment from America Online and whether

America Online might even get preferential treatment in the pages of Time magazines - which tried to bend over backwards to cover Time Warner and America Online with fairness and sometimes stinging criticism.

"Steve Case was heavily criticized from all directions when the merger happened," says respected media analyst Barry Nitwin. "A lot of people had very legitimate concerns of conflict of interest issues. Remember this is America and we're supposed to have freedom of the press. How can you have that with a big media monopoly? But it seems that Case has no desire to change the editorial direction or content of his new acquisitions. It's a good business deal for him. He's shown that he's determined to run the business side of things and to let the rest of the business run just as usual."

Norman Pearlstine, the editor in chief of Time Inc., said he trusted Case and was less worried about interference from America Online than he was about losing the distribution of corporate dollars for a new television network. "Steve Case has been saying that where it makes sense, we will do deals, but where it does not, we will not," Pearlstine said. "How does one convince Wall Street that investing in a new magazine is better than say, expanding a cable system?"

Case didn't need the Time Warner deal to solidify his place in the annals of financial history. AOL was an economic heavyweight long before the deal, with a market valuation of $130 billion. "He wanted to take it to another level, a level where nobody before him has dared to go," said Mark Benson. "The world stood still when the merger deal was announced. The dollar amounts being thrown around were so high that I don't think anybody to this day really understands the potential worth of the deal. It's frightening."

Even his harshest critics praised Case for the mega merger. Respected The Standard.com Internet columnist James Fallows said that Case had made history. "It is a moment of arrival for the Internet that we will remember years from now," Fallows said. "By extension, AOL's victory is the Internet Economy's victory...Case's company has not just revenues but large profits, making it unrepresentative of Net firms as a whole...The AOL-

Time Warner deal should be seen as the event in which the boom economy of the early 21st century came to resemble the boom economy of 100 years earlier."

Steve Case was born and raised in Hawaii. The beauty of the islands, however, was lost on young Case, who preferred reading science fiction to surfing. Despite being studious, he was not the student most likely to succeed. His school friends agree. They remember him as being shy and introverted. A bit of an oddball.

"He was always friendly and had a good head on his shoulders," said Andrew Taylor, who grew up near Case. "But I don't think anybody who knew him then could have any idea of the success he would have later on. I'm sure if you ask him he'd be the first to admit that he couldn't have predicted it himself."

Case's demeanor is that of the typical youthful, eccentric computer nerd a la Bill Gates. Like Gates, ten years ago Case would have been considered to be too much of a "wimp" to be the CEO of a major international company.

"The reality is that in the old school of doing business it was all run by guys who were sharks and had very tough exteriors," says London economics professor Jacob Woodard. "If Stephen Case or Bill Gates ran a big company 10 or 20 years ago they wouldn't have had a chance of surviving. They would have been eaten alive. They're just too nerdy."

Case graduated with a degree in Political Science from Williams College. Ironically, in 1980, Case was rejected for a job at Time Inc.'s cable TV network HBO, then headed by Gerald Levin, the CEO of Time Warner when the merger was announced.

"The man who once refused to hire him is now his employee," said Mark Benson. "If there's one thing to be learned here is to never underestimate anybody. Case with all his billions in his bank often jokes about how he was once turned down by the company he came back to buy. Maybe that was his incentive in the whole deal."

After graduating Case had aspirations of starting his own business. He founded America Online as Quantum Computer Services in 1985. It went through rapid changes since its inception and continues to do so today. Originally, it was essentially an OEM service sold by Commodore, Apple and Tandy. It continues to transform daily, with numerous new acquisitions and strategic moves. Case says that he will consider any new idea that could expand AOL's presence on the Internet. "We want to position AOL as a leader," he says. "So we'll look at anything. We're less concerned with the piece parts, and more with unifying them into an experience for the consumer."

Case bases his success mainly on one aspect of his business, customer service. He recognizes that no matter how good or interesting the product is it doesn't have a chance to survive without proper customer support. "Content isn't king. Context isn't king. Technology isn't king," he says. "The customer is king, and the customer wants everything packaged together into a single convenient service with lots of options. We have that. We have a mix of distribution, content and technology infrastructure. We have the largest footprint."

Case insists that he tries to never lets his ego interfere with making the right business decisions. "It could hurt your business badly," he says. "You just have to step aside and let the people who are qualified to make decisions. You can't know everything. That's why it's so important to surround yourself with strong people."

Many of Case's colleagues recognize how level headed he is. "AOL has the best management team in the industry," John Sidgmore said. "When Bob Pittman became No.2 at AOL Case gave him much of the power. So they didn't have ego concerns. They will work well together."

There have been moments, however, when Case doesn't see eye-to-eye with the experts he hired. Once such incident was back in June 1996 when, after only four months on the job. AOL president William Razzouk resigned. The 48-year-old Razzouk, who had an impeccable track record at Federal Express, was hired by Case to restore some order at AOL, which was facing stiff competition and controversy over its billing practices. AOL's spin doctors claimed Razzouk's family decided

54

they didn't want to move from Memphis and the Steve Case wanted to take a more hands-on role. But several AOL executives said there was more to it. "There was a lot of personality clashes between Razzouk and Case," the executive said. "Razzouk had a completely different agenda and Case and his support staff took offense to it. One of the reasons Case has been so successful is that he doesn't put up with any bullshit. If you don't perform up to his expectations you will be out the door just as fast as you got in."

Case says that the key to successful e-commerce is staying on top of things. "Things change by the second in the high-tech world," he says, "you've got to stay ahead of the competition or else you'll be in trouble. And to stay ahead you've got to take chances." One of Case's typical high risk adventures happened in June 2000, when America Online announced its plan to start selling AOLTV, an interactive programming service for televsion sets. The new service incorporates many of the features of AOL for computers, such as e-mail and web browsing. Case's major competitor is Microsoft's

WebTV, which started 3 ½ years prior to AOL. Many experts, however, were skeptical. Case's new venture might only be pie-in-the-sky hopes because WebTV had only attracted about a million subscribers despite large subsidies and heavy advertising campaigns, prompting Microsoft to develop another version that was perceived to be more TV daring, Ultimate TV.

Television newspaper columnist Eric Dixon said Case might have overestimated the potential customers from AOL's massive subscriber base of more than 23 million users worldwide. "I'd be surprised if the project fails because Case always manages to dig himself out of a hole," Dixon said. "But just because AOL has so many millions of users it doesn't automatically mean that they'll go for the new TV plan. Microsoft had the same thinking and their TV plan has failed miserably. But Case does not throw money around for nothing. He must firmly believe that this is the way to go for the future."

But Case refuses to look back after making major business decisions. He says once you decide to do something "you either sink or swim". "Our strategy has been in place for more than a decade," he says. "The goal has always been to build a mass medium that is as important in everyday life as the telephone or television. How we execute the strategy has always been in flux."

<u>4</u>

CraigBarrett

The day Andrew Grove announced he would step down from the CEO position at Intel in March 1998, Craig Barrett made it his mission to develop a distinctive trademark for a company that is to microprocessors what McDonald's is to fast food.

When Barrett arrived for his new job at Intel he knew it wouldn't be easy. He prepared himself to take on the challenge of heading a company that racks up more than $1 billion a month, 50 percent of its business, over the Internet.

The first thing Barrett wanted to do was to make sure his employees and the public understood that he was not content riding on Grove's coattails. He made it clear that the days of Intel channeling most of its energy and investment on PC chips were a thing of the past. He started reshaping Intel into a supplier of all kinds of semiconductors for networking gear, information appliances and PCs. But that wasn't enough. He introduced Intel into e-commerce, Internet servers, consumer electronics and wireless phones. He committed to spending $1 billion during a two-year period on developing one of the world's most sophisticated Internet data facilities.

Barrett put himself on the line. He succeeded Grove not content to rest on past accomplishments. "We're putting a new image on top of the big powerful chip monster that eats the world," he said.

Barrett's new vision received rave reviews from both employees and the media. It was in marked contrast to his predecessor Grove who was often the target of criticism.

Before making any big decision Barrett pores over piles of statistical information specific to its target audience. "I like to work quickly and efficiently," he says. "If something doesn't add up then I don't mind waiting to do it until it makes sense."

Barrett became the fourth CEO since Intel's founding in 1968. Barrett's philosophy from Grove's is much different. Grove's legendary management slogan was "Only the paranoid survive". Barrett's is a much more conservative "hard work pays off". And during his short tenure Barrett has shown that he's bent on eclipsing the Grove's legacy.

"In such a short time he's taken Intel into directions that the company had not previously considered," says Silicon Valley financial analyst Gordon Parkes. "Most of Intel's top executives were taken aback by Barrett's new plan. They had all been used to dealing in computer chips. But Barrett realized that times have changed and that more focus would have to be placed on e-commerce. And in the process of this change investors have been enthusiastic. Barrett's plans have not tightened the companies' bank account."

Although Barrett's innovative ideas were greeted enthusiastically in most circles, Internet analysts say there were not many other choices. After ten years of 30 percent plus compound annual growth, Intel started to have major problems by 1998. Grove's attempts to expand into new markets such as video conferencing and wireless communications reached a dead end. Increased competition and new low prices for PCs didn't help. Intel's revenue growth faltered to a disappointing five percent. To make matters worse Intel's stock went down almost 40 percent. Barrett realized that the PC business was not as lucrative as it had been a few years back.

"Because of the price wars among PC clone manufacturers Intel lost billions of dollars," says Internet financial journalist Peter Menke. "Barrett knew that he had to reshape the company to keep up with the times. The PC had become overshadowed by the Internet. The new low cost PC clones meant low cost chips. This was not good at all for Intel."

Within days of filling Grove's seat in May, 1998, Barrett began shaking up the administration Grove left behind. The first thing he did was loosen up Grove's tight centralized management structure, eventually reshaping Intel into five groups whose managers were obligated to report to him. Like many other computer giants for the first time in 1999 Intel spent more on buying start up companies than it did on research and development and equipment. Intel bought twelve companies for an estimated $6 billion.

"Never before have I seen one individual take over a big company and shake it to its foundation in such short a time," said Peter Menke. "Barrett really put his job on the line. Many people at Intel were initially worried but they took comfort in Barrett's cool, friendly approach. Grove was a tyrant, a throwback to the type of boss who instilled fear in his employees. Barrett is the total opposite."

Barrett's background, like his management style, is much different than Grove's. He grew up in an affluent family in San Francisco and attended Stanford University from 1957-1964, receiving his Bachelor of Science, Master of Science and Ph.D. degrees in Materials Science. He was offered several good jobs after graduation but decided to remain at Stanford, where he joined the faculty in the Department of Materials Science and Engineering. Barrett was well respected by both faculty and students and rose to the position of associate professor. He was a Fulbright Fellow at the Danish Technical University in Denmark in 1972 and a NATO Postdoctoral Fellow at the National Physical Laboratory in England in 1964. In 1969 Barrett received the Hardy Gold Medal from the American Institue of Mining and Metallurgical Engineers, an award which helped him acquire international claim.

"I like traveling and meeting people from different cultures," Barrett says. "It's a great educational experience. It was a great thrill to win those awards. It was a very exciting time in my life."

Barrett stayed at Stanford until 1974, when he joined Intel as a Technology Development Manager. Intel's management had been eyeing Barrett for a while but could not steal him away because of Barrett's commitment to Stanford. "Craig wanted to fulfill his commitments to Stanford," recalls one of Barrett's longtime close friends. "That's the type of person he is. He's not an opportunist like most other guys in the high-tech industry who just jump at the next best financial opportunity. He believes in allegiance because he was brought up in a family that preached honesty. Craig had so many offers because he was one of the brightest young men for the job at the time. Obviously he made the right choice with Intel."

Grove is more of a rags to riches story. He came to America in 1957 with almost not a penny in his pocket. He spoke little English and was so poor that he had to survive on just about bread and water during the first few months. His first years in America were very tough. He had to endure the hard struggles that most new immigrants were forced to face during that time.

Years later, when he stepped down as CEO in 1998, Grove's estimated worth was more than $300 million. He had achieved what most new immigrants in

America can only dream of. He left a mark on the financial world that is among the most far reaching achievements of any of his contemporaries. Many high-tech industry moguls agree that without Grove things in the computer industry might never have grown so fast.

"Grove is all about the American Dream," says former Intel employee Alan Wilson. "He had to work extremely hard for everything he got in life. Maybe that's why he was so strict with his employees. He was real old school. But he was an innovator who turned Intel into an international powerhouse company. Barrett comes from an education background and is very well versed on how to deal with today's breed of employees. He doesn't try to hold as much as a firm grip as Grove. And it has worked splendidly. People look forward to going to work for Barrett. Many dreaded and feared Grove."

When Grove gave the throne to Barrett many people speculated that it was for health reasons. Grove had been treated for prostate cancer a couple of years earlier. Grove, however, said that was not the case.

"I need to concentrate on other aspects of the business," Grove said. "It's time, Craig Barrett is ready, and I'm ready." Immediately after stepping down Grove made it clear that he wasn't about to retire. He seemed to work harder than ever, giving speeches around the world and focusing on the challenge of making sure Intel's expansion under Barrett was smooth.

"Most people in Grove's position would have just walked out with all their millions and never come back," says Alan Wilson. "I think everybody was amazed by how hard Grove was working. He was in such demand on the lecture circuit that he was booked almost two years in advance. Things were as hectic as ever for Andrew."

Grove said his new duties allowed him to spend more time concentrating on promoting Intel to key business people and the public. When he was CEO, he said, he found himself spending more than half of his time in staff meetings and on the telephone. "The change was due because at this point I was more valuable to the company in other areas," Grove said. "We're a disciplined company. And to some extent, as chief executive you become beholden to that scheduling discipline. Now, I want to be able to go where my interest takes me. And my interest is market growth."

When Barrett replaced Grove the average selling price of Intel's microprocessors had been about $235 a chip for most of the previous decade. Today the average price is about $150, which is the primary reason why Barrett decided to branch out Intel's business structure. In such a short time Barrett's exploits and friendly personality have hypnotized his peers. All over the high-tech industry Barrett's colleagues are trying to divine the source of his magic. They want to know how, in two short years, he increased revenue in 1999 to $29.4 billion, up 12 percent from 1998. They want to know how he has solidified Intel once again as the forerunner in building chips, this time aimed at a new market for wireless devices and networks that link users to the Web from anywhere they might be, including their cars, offices or bathrooms. Though he does little to encourage it, Barrett's renown is spreading.

"If there was one guy I would pick to be a CEO today Craig would be at the top of the list," says Wall Street broker Bruce Rush. "He's got more experience, more intellect and more charisma than all of those young guys coming out of college and attaching a fancy CEO title to their name. Intel put itself in a can't lose position with Craig. He's so well respected. Everybody is lining up to do business with him."

The nature of Barrett's personality and methods represent the leading edge of several new economic directions for Intel. By the year 2005, Barrett's goal is for all of Intel's new ventures to be $1 billion-plus businesses and rank in the top two in their markets. He says that it will help Intel grow 20 percent a year from its dismal 8 percent compound growth when he took over. Immediate results showed his maneuvers paying huge dividends. Intel shares were up 40 percent shortly after he took over, the biggest growth among the 20 most popular stocks in America. "Craig came on board and took Intel into a whole new world," Bruce Rush says. "Intel was late to cash in on the success of the Internet but Craig made up for the lost time in his first year. The results have been remarkable."

5

Timothy Koogle

If you were cruising near Bill Gates's home across Lake Washington in Seattle and saw what might have appeared to be a swanky sports car dealership, chances were good that you'd stumbled upon the driveway of the getaway home of Yahoo CEO Timothy Koogle. Koogle, who during the week works out of Yahoo's head office in Santa Clara, California, is fondly regarded as one of the high-tech industry's most flamboyant characters. He loves parties, high-speed race cars and vintage electric guitars. But he remains well grounded, turning a company whose Internet sites include a range of features from chat rooms to news and search services into a gold mine.

"He's one of the most flamboyant characters in the business," says Internet venture capitalist John Randall. "I have never met another CEO who is anything like him. He lives life fast and according to his own set of rules. And he's also worked extremely hard for everything he's accomplished. Often, when people meet him they think that if he can become so successful anybody can. And Timothy probably says that himself. But it's important to realize that this man is a workaholic. Success didn't come so easy for him. He's had to work his ass off."

The story of Timothy Koogle is in essence, the story of the success of Yahoo and the high-tech industry today. When he was 7, it became apparent that Koogle was headed for great business success when he started working for his father who was a mechanic and machinist. His father taught him how to build engines. Young Timothy made more money than any of his friends at school by rebuilding the engines of people's cars in his hometown Alexandria, Virginia. In the early seventies,

72

Koogle says his years as an undergraduate at the University of Virginia's engineering school gave him a solid foundation because most of his professors had been accomplished engineers.

"They brought their real-world experience into the classroom and showed us the applications of the technology we were studying," Koogle recalled. "I got really stoked about it."

After Virginia, Koogle got a master's degree and a Ph.D. in engineering from Stanford. It was at Stanford where Koogle first got his feet wet in the business world. He started two companies, one of which he eventually sold out to his partners. His other business made controllers for electronics manufacturing. He sold the business to Motorola, where he worked for nine years in its operations and venture capital groups. At Motorola, Koogle learned the in-and-outs of making big deals. He was responsible for placing millions of dollars into promising business plans by promising start-up companies. He was forced to become a man.

"Timothy was young, bright and very determined to succeed," recalled Alex Shaw, a former Motorola executive. "He was also very respected. In those days it wasn't common to let a young kid make decisions that involved millions of dollars. It wasn't like today where you see kids 25 and 26 making crucial decisions. Timothy was an exception. When you talked to him it was like you were talking to somebody who had been in the business more than twenty years. He kept himself very well briefed."

After Motorola, Koogle was recruited by Seattle's Intermec as chief engineer and later president. He made his mark quickly. During his three years at the data communications product maker Koogle was credited with increasing sales by more than 50 percent from $125 million to $350 million. When Koogle arrived at Intermec, then a financially strapped subsidiary of the big bar-code maker Raytheon, many people were skeptical. Barely thirty, many of Koogle's co-workers thought he was too young.

"It was a risky move," said Eric Neimann, an engineer who knew Koogle. "There's no doubt that Timothy was one of the brightest in the business but many people wondered if he was old enough to command the respect of a large staff. He also didn't dress like the typical president of a company. He would often be in a t-shirt and jeans, not the kind of president companies were used to in those days. Timothy probably revolutionized the change in clothing attire in offices around the world. Many people started copying him."

Yahoo made waves in the high-tech industry in August 1995, when Koogle took over as the company's CEO. Yahoo's board of directors interviewed a half-dozen candidates for the post before settling on Koogle. Koogle, now in his mid forties, looked more like an aging rock 'n roller. He was a logical choice. Although he was years older than the other employees at Yahoo, where the average age was 29, he still had a youthful exuberance.

"When I first met him he seemed like he was still a kid," said one board member. "His outlook was fresh and very positive. And he didn't seem to have an ego. I knew he was the right man for the position."

"He's very decisive and very focused," said another board member, Michael Moritz. "But he's also very approachable. He's the type of guy who doesn't make the people around him feel uncomfortable."

Koogle became Yahoo's sixth employee. The company's co-founders who were graduates of Stanford were impressed with Koogle's long term vision. Jerry Yang, David Filo and Chief Operating Officer Jeffrey Mallett had not considered making exploring advertising on their site until Koogle arrived.

"They were more interested in the freewheeling culture of the Internet," said Internet Investment analyst Dick Young. "They had a great idea but needed direction on how to make money with it. When Koogle came on board he showed them how to make money from the get go. He was the missing puzzle to the management team. Once Koogle took over things started to happen for Yahoo faster than anybody could have ever imagined. It just goes to show you that no matter how good one's business idea is it will go nowhere unless the right people are hired."

Koogle, who's no slouch when it comes to pranks and partying, was more level headed than many of his colleagues at Yahoo. He shied away from engaging in some of the fun and games that earned Yahoo the reputation for being as one New York critic wrote "a 9-5 playground". When Yahoo went public in 1996, founders Jerry Yang and David Filo were officially "Chief Yahoos". Koogle firmly refused to take on the title of "Chief Chief Yahoo". He also declined to tattoo the company logo on his rear end like another top executive. And he steadfastly refused a request from Business Week to spray-paint his wild gray head of hair in purple and Yellow, Yahoo's company colors.

"Without Koogle it would have taken Yahoo a lot longer to succeed because there was too much fun and games there," said New York Internet financial analyst Steven Day. "Koogle is a bit of a prankster himself but as soon as he got on board he realized that he needed to take a mature attitude to balance the company. He made a wise decision. While the other employees joked around Koogle made crucial decisions and earned the respect of his co-workers. Everybody looked up to him for advice and leadership."

Yahoo's management team was firmly intact. Yang played the gung-ho long term planner, Filo the computer whiz, Mallett the all round operations manager and Koogle the experienced decision maker. "It was like filling in all the holes on a sports team," Yang said. "We put the right people in the right place. We had a mix of youth with a mix of veterans. We felt we had a championship team."

Building Yahoo into a profitable company came for Koogle came just as easy as rebuilding car engines. Yahoo reported its first profitable quarter in September 1997 and never looked back. For example in Winter 1999, Yahoo reported an operating profit of $28 million. Shares of Yahoo surged as much as $8.5625, to $217, in after-hours trading. Earnings were 11 cents a share, shattering Wall Street forecast of 8 cents a share. Koogle promised that Yahoo would continue to move in the same direction, making major acquisitions with "no near-term" plan to put its money into non-Internet assets like television media companies.

"Koogle makes sure that his employees don't get complacent," says Steven Day. "When the company has a good quarter he doesn't sit back and relax. He immediately set new goals. And he does whatever it takes to make sure the new goals are met."

Koogle is not a free spender like many of his fellow Silicon Valley colleagues who like to live high off the hog. In fact, he's regarded as being one of the most tight fisted CEOs in the high-tech world. Executives must comply to Yahoo's company rule of not spending a cent more than they have to. If a meeting is dragging on they must wrap it up to catch the day's last flight instead of spending on a hotel room. Salaries at Yahoo are low compared to other top Internet companies. Employees, however, are rewarded with lucrative stock options. Koogle's are worth about a half billion dollars.

"The problem with most high-tech companies is that they start to think that money grows on trees," says one Yahoo engineer. "Eventually the free spending lifestyle catches up to them and cash starts to run out. That's why Yahoo is so successful and doesn't have the financial problems that so many other dot-com companies have recently had. Yahoo is very careful with its cash and doesn't throw its money around like there's no tomorrow."

Yahoo's penny-pinching attitude has not always worked to its benefit. In 1998 Yahoo desperately tried to buy its major competitor Excite. Yahoo had second thoughts about the financial conditions of the deal. Excite immediately started negotiating with At Home. At Home made Excite an irresistible offer with the condition that Yahoo would not be given a chance to make a counter offer. Excite couldn't refuse.

For Yahoo the Excite deal was a good learning experience. In its next big deal, Yahoo offered Geocities a big premium over its existing share price on the condition that Geocities agree to the deal within 24 hours. Six weeks later Yahoo made a similar offer to Broadcast.com. These deals were frowned upon by

Yahoo's investors. Advertisers were not receptive to both Geocities and Broadcast.com's pages.

"Yahoo was looking more at the big picture," says Internet analyst Steven Day. "In hindsight the deals made sense. But for immediate results it didn't work out the way they expected. Yahoo poured a lot of cash into those deals and they weren't getting the immediate return they projected."

Some 100 million people worldwide visit Yahoo each month, which attracts Yahoo's advertising revenue of more than half a billion dollars. But most Internet analysts agree that Yahoo could soon be in danger because of the highly publicized AOL Time Warner merger. Koogle is under enormous pressure to come up with something that will keep Yahoo on the same playing surface as AOL Time Warner. Liz Buyer, an analyst at Credit Suisse First Boston, speculated that Yahoo would be forced to give up its independent status and buy brand name consumer content like Fortune magazines and Sports Illustrated from Time Warner to keep up with AOL. Rumors of a deal with Rupert Murdoch's News

Corp., cyber-auction, eBay, have also surfaced. But Koogle doesn't want to speculate.

"We partner with a lot of companies, grow the things that work and shoot the things that don't. We've done business with the people at News Corp. and will continue to do so but I can't predict anything beyond that," Koogle said.

Yahoo has also made news for reasons that Koogle would like to forget. On May 22, 2000 a French judge ruled that Yahoo had broken French law and committed "an offense to the collective memory" of the country by allowing online auctions of neo-Nazi objects in cyberspace. Yahoo was given two months to find a way to make the site inaccessible to Internet users in France and to pay $1,390 each to the Union of Jewish Students and an anti-racism group. Yahoo responded to the court's decision by saying it "condemned all forms of racism". But the company conceeds that the case raised questions about responsibility on the Internet.

"The real question put before this court is whether a French jurisdiction can make a decision on the English content of an American site, run by an American company...for the sole reason that French users have access via the Internet," Yahoo lawyer Christophe Pecnard said.

Yahoo's credibility took a beating. International human rights activists were outraged. "It seems to me that Yahoo is trying to distance itself from taking the blame," said an Oxford human rights scholar. "The bottom line is that they provided the outlet to sell very offensive material. They should be held accountable. The ruling was a victory. It will force Yahoo to avoid incidents like this in the future."

Meanwhile, Koogle continues to push ahead, no matter what obstacles lie in his way. After the ruling in France he said that Yahoo would be more careful in the future. He has also, according to several people at Yahoo, been working harder than ever to try to keep Yahoo up with an Internet that changes by the second.

"There are lots of people in Silicon Valley who start and end with 'How do I make lots of money?' I'm not about that," Koogle said in an interview. "I'm into building businesses and making money...I can't even imagine retiring and sitting on a beach somewhere. I'll probably retire the day I die."

6

S teven J obs

Steven Jobs represents the end-product of the rise of Silicon Valley that has set the standard for the world's high-tech industry. He is a compulsive achiever who revolutionized computers long before the world had ever heard of Bill Gates. He became legendary for his daredevil exploits and unconventional lifestyle that seemed to take him over the edge of normal life. He is also known to take risks and gamble on new and unproven technology. He dated Joan Baez and had Ella Fitzgerald sing at his 30th birthday party. Jobs has led quite the life!

"That's why he's so successful," says former Apple employee Stanley Duke. "Steve never followed anybody's agenda but his own. He was determined to do something different than everybody else. That is the key to being successful. And he has integrity. Most people in the computer business are more interested in quantity than quality. Steve has an impeccable aesthetic sense. He doesn't put out garbage for the sake of making a buck like many of his competitors have done."

For Steve Jobs, creativity has been more than anything the force that keeps him going in a world of endless business meetings, late nights and 85-hour weeks. It was only a few years ago that Apple seemed doomed to the PC world until Jobs came back to the rescue. Jobs felt compelled to do something to save Apple's sinking ship. Jobs, the computer industry's number one product design denizen, cut costs and offered shareholders with an astonishing more than 650 percent increase in Apple's market value, to $17 billion.

"Any person starting thinking about starting a business should study Steve Jobs," says Wall Street analyst Peter Whilst. "He looks and acts like an artist but he's also a shrewd businessman. He's in a league of his own. He's been the target of much envy and criticism over the years but his place in history is very secure. Nobody did more than Steve Jobs to change the use of the home computer and I'm sure even Bill Gates would agree."

Jobs' success is remarkable considering his turbulent family background. From the day he was born, Jobs had to cope with the fact that his biological parents put him up for adoption. At the time his parents, who were unmarried, were financially stable but weren't ready to raise a child. His father, a political science professor, convinced his mother, a speech therapist to put their baby up for adoption - a decision they would deeply regret for the rest of their lives. Jobs's biological sister, Mona Simpson, was born two and a half years later. Simpson, today a well-known novelist, was shocked some 27 years later when Jobs tracked her down. "Steve was obsessed from the time he was 12 years old to find his real family, like is so often the case with adopted children," journalist

Craig Wilson said. "Steve spent years tracking down his family. He needed to find out why his parents decided to put him up for adoption. It was the one thing in life that confused him more than anything."

Jobs had a middle-class upbringing with his adopted parents, Clara, an accountant and Paul Jobs, a machinist for a company that was a leader in manufacturing lasers. They adopted Steve in 1956. Clara and Paul raised little Steve in Los Altos, California. Both are now deceased. Steve refers to them as his real parents and says they did a formidable job raising him. He remembers Paul as being a great craftsman, a "genius with his hand." Steve says Paul bought cars for $50 that were nothing more than beat up jalopies and gave them complete overhauls. He would sell them to students, earning a nice profit that he saved up to put Steve through college. "My parents were great people," Jobs said. "I want to be as good to my children as my parents were to me."

Sociologist Richard Tanner says that Jobs would not have been as successful without his adoptive parents.

88

"I've seen so many cases where the adopted children become ambivalent towards their adopted parents. It could create a lot of emotional problems in the future," Tanner said. "But there are also wonderful stories like that of Steve Jobs. It's obvious that he had some problems early on but his adopted parents were wonderful people. Steve eventually tracked down his real family for his own personal reasons but it wasn't because his adopted parents did a poor job. It was probably more out of curiosity. Steve turned out to be the success he is today because of the way he was raised by his adopted parents."

Growing up in Silicon Valley for Steve was tantamount to an astronaut growing up on the moon. Steve watched with great curiosity the groundwork of the personal computer industry being put together. Ever since he was a boy Steve had aspirations of working in the high-tech field.

At school Steve was known as a troublemaker. He was one of the least popular kids in his class and showed little interest in academics. He was withdrawn. "He was an enigma," recalls an old classmate. "He had a head on his shoulders but he didn't seem to want to use it. He was a bit of a crybaby. He didn't fit in with the other kids. When he'd be asked to do something with the other kids he'd throw a fit and cry. The other kids stayed away from him because they thought he was weird."

His teachers agree with that assessment. In an eerie similarity to Albert Einstein, Steve had the potential to be the smartest kid in the class but his teachers said he was reluctant to perform. In grade four his behavior became so erratic that his teacher expelled him from the class. Another teacher took him in, a move that turned Steve around. Today, Steve recalls that the teacher found a way to motivate students like Steve. She offered them incentives, including money. Steve became obsessed with overachieving so that he could cash out. He skipped grade five. Crittenden Junior High School, located in a rough neighborhood near the Bay, was a rough experience for Steve. There were too many troublemakers. Fights broke out daily and many of the students carried knives. The year before Steve enrolled several grade eight boys were arrested for gang rape. A year later, Steve's parents moved to a more safer area in Sunnyvale. They had to get Steve out of Crittenden's rough environment. Sunnyvale was one of the first neighborhoods to be integrated into Silicon Valley. Most of its residents worked in high-tech.

Steve was determined to succeed. When he was only 12, Steve worked up the courage to call Hewlett-Packard president William Hewlett at his home in Palo Alto. Steve needed various parts for a frequency counter he was building. During his youth, Steve spent more time building high-tech gadgets than he did anything else. It was his passion. Hewlett was impressed with young Steve and not only agreed to send him the parts but also offered him a summer job at the company that was the pioneer of Silicon Valley.

"There weren't too many 12 year olds who would have the guts to make a phone call like that," says longtime Silicon Valley engineer Tom Silver. "That's why Steve Jobs is so successful. He's never been afraid to take chances. The worst that could have happened is that William Hewlett would have said a resounding no. But that one phone call opened up a whole new opportunity for Steve. It's a lesson to be learned. In business the worst thing to do is to be afraid of rejection."

Steve's parents had always wanted him to get a university degree. In 1972, after attending Reed College in Portland, Oregon, he dropped out after only one semester because he "needed more spiritual enlightenment". He bummed around Portland for the rest of the year, hanging out with musicians, hippies and free spirits immersed in Portland's alternative culture. But he quickly tired of that bohemian existence. Living a hand-to-mouth existence was not enough for Jobs. He needed to extract more from life. He worried that he was turning into a bum. He needed something that would earn him more respect and cash.

Steve finally decided to do something that inspired him more than anything else in life - working with computers. He realized that his future could only be tinkering with obscure computer components, trying to build something incredible. He spent hours on end teaching himself how to program and to build new components. Why should he sit in some stuffy University classroom when he could be doing what he did best, fiddling with computers, he often wondered.

In 1974 Jobs was hired as a video game designer for Atari. He worked there for several months before he felt the need for more spirituality. This quest would take him to India with a close friend from Reed College, Dan Kottke.

"Like most people his age, Steve Jobs was in search of something incredible," said sociologist Evan Dean, who has conducted several studies on Jobs and on the effects of the high-tech industry on modern society. "He was torn because he was somewhat of a free spirit and he wasn't yet ready to commit himself to working in an ivory tower. He preferred being out there with real people and learning some lessons in life. I'm sure today that he'd agree that his travel experiences were worth as much to him as anything else he did in his life."

When he returned from India that Fall, Jobs hooked up with an old acquaintance from his days working during the summer at Hewlett-Packard, Stephen Wozniak. Jobs started attending meetings of Wozniak's legendary "Homebrew Computer Club". Wozniak was a brilliant engineer who was always inventing new computer concepts. He inspired Jobs. Jobs and Wozniak grew to be friends and started collaborating. It was a match made in heaven. Jobs was in charge of design and marketing while Wozniak worked out the technical stuff. They decided that here might be a huge market for PC's and came up with the idea of forming Apple Computer. Together they built the first Apple I computer in Jobs's bedroom and started working out of his garage.

In June of 1976, an enthusiastic 21-year-old Jobs approached one of Silicon Valley's leading advertising agencies with a plan for marketing personal computers. The ad rep was not impressed and told Jobs that he didn't think the project had any chance to get off the ground. "Steve is young and inexperienced," the rep wrote in an internal memo to his boss. "His system sells for $666.66, but there is as yet no evidence that the retailers are successful in finding customers."

The ad rep's judgment was reminiscent of the tale of a mechanic who once told the Wright brothers that their planes would probably never get off the ground. Apple pioneered and popularized the world of desktop publishing with its pull-down menus, the mouse and graphical user-friendly interface. It also changed the image of the corporate environment. Employees came to work in jeans and t-shirts, making Apple look more like a groovy youth hostel than a powerhouse American company.

The duo had to sell some of their treasured possessions to raise seed money. Jobs sold his Volkswagon micro-bus. Wozniak sold his Hewlett-Packard scientific calculator. With $1300 raised, their new company was born. Jobs came up with the name Apple as a tribute to the most enjoyable summer he had when he worked in an apple orchard in Oregon.

Jobs and Wozniak's Apple I became an instant hit. It brought them $774,000 in sales. The next year the pair developed Apple II, which had internal built-in circuitry allowing the computer to interact with a color video monitor. It was the birth of the programming industry. Independent programmers recognized the limitless potential and invented some 20,000 new software programs. Within three years, Apple II posted earnings of $139,000,000, a remarkable growth of 700 percent. In 1980 Apple went public. Shares of $22 the first day immediately shot up to $29. Apple's market value was now $1.2 billion. By 1982, Apple had sales of $583,000,000, a 74 percent increase from the previous year. There was no end in sight.

Meanwhile Jobs lived the high life. He was romantically linked to folk icon Joan Baez and became a mainstay on the Hollywood party scene. The man who once felt like a pariah in society was now on the A list of the most famous people in the world. He still preferred dressing in jeans and running shoes, but his colorful lifestyle was not anywhere near that of the average American. He bought fancy sports cars, big homes and was constantly spotted in the company of Hollywood's most desirable women.

"He was now the most important and eligible man in the world," says gossip columnist Rita Brown. "He was more eligible than any Prince or billionaire. The world became fascinated with Steve Jobs and women dreamt of being near him or winding up in his arms. Nobody in business since Howard Hughes had become such a mystique to the public and media."

Many of Jobs's colleagues resented his carefree way of life. In January 1984, Jobs quoted a line from Bob Dylan's song "The Times They Are A-Changin" before demonstrating the revolutionary Macintosh personal computer to Apple's board of directors. The Macintosh was Jobs's pet project. He was excited that his invention became the premium tool for the music and entertainment industry. "I loved it because all kinds of cool people I respected were using it," he once said.

A year later, however, Jobs was forced out by Apple's board. They perceived Jobs as too much of a visionary. Without Jobs Apple's more than $10 billion in annual revenue sunk rapidly. In hindsight Apple's board made a fatal error rebelling against Jobs, who was

97

responsible for a long line of outstanding products, including Quicktime software and the powerbook line of portable Macintosh's. "People were jealous of Jobs and they started getting very greedy," says Silicon Valley analyst Andrew Weiner. "In business you must put egos and pride aside. Otherwise you become more prone to failure."

The most outspoken person against Jobs is John Scully, the former Pepsi Cola mogul who Jobs recruited as Apple's new president. Many former Apple employees say that Scully was extremely jealous of Jobs's fame and portrayed Jobs as an undesirable to the board to get him out of the way.

"Scully used the excuse that Jobs's spending was too high and that he was too liberal in his ways," one employee said. "but I think that Scully got tired of playing second fiddle. What happens so often in business happened to Jobs. The man he once hired was now trying to get him fired. It was a sheer power struggle." Jobs was only 30 when he left Apple with $150 million in his pocket. Money, however, couldn't assuage some of the hurt and betrayal he felt.

But Jobs's legacy could not be erased. Even Bill Gates was one of his biggest fans. He was so impressed with Macintosh's operating system that he emulated it with his Microsoft's Windows operating system. Gates was overcome with emotion at a 1983 conference when Jobs introduced the Macintosh to Apple's national sales force. Jobs's oratory left everyone in the room standing on chairs and screaming. "The emotion in that room was

a beach resort and drinking Jobs bounced back quickly. m the film director George illion. Jobs invested $50 kar, which produced several isney. The deal paid off. ox office smash of 1995.
yet to come. By the mid vay behind PCs and was stay afloat. Rumors about

[Handwritten note overlaying the text:]

Staples

* Planner
* Pen with good
* pt.
* Weekly
monthly
quaterly
siren you
* Burl o Powers

the company's demise were rampant. In December 1996 Apple announced that its co-founder Jobs would return to the company he resigned from 11 years ago. Apple also purchased Jobs's company, Next Software Inc., for $350 million in cash and stock and assumed nearly $50 million in debt. Jobs special title was adviser to the chairman Gilbert F. Amelio. "The more we talked the more we realized this was a tremendously great relationship," Amelio told reporters.

Less than a year later Jobs made a move that stunned the computer world. He persuaded his longtime rival Bill Gates to inject $150 million in Apple. Apple users were infuriated and deemed Jobs a traitor. "What he did is the same as it would be if the U.S. paid for Fidel Castro's cigars," said die-hard Mac user Jason Woodson. "We felt that Jobs had sold out. Mac users have lots of pride. Now we felt that we had fallen into the hands of the enemy, Bill Gates."

Despite all the criticism, once again, Jobs proved that he is indeed a business genius. After running up losses totaling $1.86 billion in 1996 and 1997 Gilbert

Amelio was ousted as the head of Apple. Jobs was appointed temporary CEO. Initially Jobs insisted that he didn't want the position full-time because of family commitments. He once said that "spending 150 hours a week in an office ruined my first marriage". At 41, Jobs felt he didn't need the headache. As soon as he became CEO again, however, Jobs caught the work bug. He was determined to rebuild Apple. But the opportunities were different now. Nobody expected him to have much of a chance. The sales of personal computers were not what they once had been. The high-tech world was now focused on the future, which became the world of wired and wireless hand-held consumer electronic products.

Jobs, however, had a plan. With his genius for design, he introduced Apple's futuristic iMac computer. After cleaning up some of its flaws, iMac put Apple back on the map. It became Apple's most popular product in years. Sales soared! By 1999, Apple had silenced its harshest critics, posting its sixth consecutive profitable quarter. It had held more than 12 percent of the retail and mail-order PC market for its last two quarters. For the first time in years, Apple was back in the top five manufacturers of personal computers in the world.

"If Apple had not gotten rid of Steve Jobs in 1985 there might not be any Bill Gates today," says Wall Street analyst Louise Berman. "It was the dumbest move ever. Nobody knows the business better than Jobs. Other people were jealous of him and obviously egos got in the way. But he's back and he's really the only person who I think Bill Gates is really afraid of. That's the reason why Gates invested in Apple. If you can't beat em join em."

While Jobs continues to spearhead Apple's revival he remains the CEO of Pixar. He shuttles back and forth by helicopter from Pixar in Richmond, California, to Apple in Cupertino. Pixar released Toy Story 2 to box office records last year, grossing almost $300 million. And he's managed to reach a new generation with iMac. One third of iMac users are first time computer buyers, and a large percentage of them are 18-25 years old. "He made a brilliant decision going for kids right out of college," says computer columnist George Rhodes. "He put Mac back on the map. The man's a genius. He keeps up with the times."

Until Mac fully recovers, Jobs draws a salary of $1.00 a year from Apple. But don't be fooled, Jobs is more wealthy than ever. He's compensated in other ways. Apple's board of directors bought him a $40 million Gulfstream V jet and his stock options are estimated to be worth billions. His 65 percent share of Pixar is worth more than $1 billion. Not too shabby for a college dropout who started out of his garage!

7

Margaret Whitman

A teenage girl and her father were gazing at the posters announcing the 2000 Bloomberg Internet Conference in San Francisco. Some of the Internet's top heavyweights were listed as guest speakers, including AOL president Robert Pittman and Yahoo's co-founder Jerry Yang. Below Yang's name was Margaret Whitman, eBay's president and CEO.

"I had no idea a woman was the CEO of eBay," Barry Gordon said to his daughter Cheryl, who aspires to one day run an Internet company like Whitman. "Meg's my hero," Cheryl replied. "I know all about her. I've even sent her a couple of emails telling her how much of a great job she's doing and I received replies. If there's any woman I admire, it's Meg."

Margaret C. Whitman was greeted with both delight and dismay when she took over the CEO duties from eBay founder Pierre Omidyar in May 1998. Although she was legendary for being one of the world's most successful consumer products marketing mavens, many experts doubted she could handle heading the Internet's most notorious auction companies, eBay.

"A lot of people shook their head in disbelief when Whitman got the eBay job," says New York business writer Alan Driessen. "Unlike other Internet companies eBay's job criteria is different. You need to have an outstanding knowledge of working online aside from a great business background. Whitman did not have that kind of track record. And the fact that she's a woman didn't help. The eBay site tends to be male dominated and the argument was made strongly by many eBay users that it would have been better to appoint a man."

When Margaret Whitman was approached by a headhunter in November 1997 to leave her lucrative job at Hasbro Inc. promoting Teletubbies, her answer was a resoudning "no". The offer to become the CEO of a then unknown Silicon Valley Internet startup company did not appeal to her at all. She loved living in Boston with her husband and two sons and had aspirations of continuing up the corporate ladder at Hasbro. Out of sheer curiosity Whitman agreed to visit eBay's headquarters in San Jose. At least, she thought, she would walk away with a mini vacation.

But the day she set foot in eBay's cramped offices her life completely changed. She was sold. After a week of meetings with company executives, venture capitalists and testimonials from devout eBay users Whitman decided she would have to be nuts to turn it down. "I thought something was very right here," she told the New York Times. "They had touched a consumer nerve."

Whitman and her family quickly packed up and headed to California. Her first task was to prepare eBay for its initial public stock offering, something Pierre Omidyar had dreamt of since the day eBay first opened its doors. Robert Kagle, a partner at eBay venture capital backer Benchmark Capital, said he felt the future of eBay was contingent on hiring Whitman.

"I was looking for a brand builder to help make eBay a household name," Kagle said. "Understanding technology was not the central ingredient. You have to get the emotional component of the customer experience in your gut."

Today, nobody can argue that Whitman wasn't the ideal choice. Pierre Omidyar's intuition was impeccable. Before Whitman, eBay relied mostly on word of mouth advertising to attract sellers and buyers. Whitman came on board with a vision to start advertising. She devised new ways of getting people to click on eBay, including targeting hobbyists in a particular field and popular target groups such as senior citizens.

"Before Meg joined eBay it was still a limited operation," Omidyar said from eBay's headquarters in San Jose, California. "She uses her marketing and business expertise to branch eBay out into markets that were once considered unattainable. She injected great energy and a completely new direction into the company. And its paid off very well."

There is nothing wrong with the worship of the famous's wealth and glamour, it's truly a favorite American pastime. But because of her success at eBay Whitman receives just as much or more interview requests from the media like entertainers and athletes, such as Madonna and Pete Sampras. Its difficult for her to walk down the street without being spotted. She is recognized wherever she goes.

Recently, a waitress at a Los Angeles restaurant asked her an autograph. A furniture mover recognized her from a TV talkshow and asked for an autograph for his wife. She's joined the "Giga-star" ranks of Bill Gates and Larry Ellison.

"She's even more popular than them," says TV producer Lance Howarth. "She could pick and choose whatever show she wants to be on. Everybody wants her. She's a treasure. EBay doesn't have to pay a dime anymore for publicity. All that they have to do is put Meg on publicity tours."

109

Working for eBay gave Whitman a bona fide chance of making more money than she could have ever imagined. Although her base salary was only $175,000 plus bonuses in 1998, Whitman was given options to buy a split-adjusted 7.2 million shares at 7 cents each. She exercised all of them to get stock then valued at $6 per share around the time eBay went public in September 1998. The move was a major coup, bringing gains of $42.7 million as of the day she exercised the options. By March 1, 1999, Whitman's shares shot up from the $6 IPO price, earning her 17th among all CEOs and number 1 among women executives in a Business Week magazine survey of 1998 pay at 365 major companies. EBay showed how the new Internet economy could make executives into millionaires, even billionaires, in a short time. Within a year, Whitman cashed out $50 million of her stock. Business analysts agree that Whitman is a beneficiary of the new Internet economy.

"You look at people like Whitman and your head turns," says Los Angeles financial planner Jason Marsh. "A woman like her would have been lucky to make

$75,000 a year including bonuses only a three or four years ago. Today sky is the limit. If you're able to land a good job with an Internet company and get in on stock options you could cash in within a year or two. Whitman is the classic example. Let's face it, before she joined eBay she was barely a somebody. Today she's mentioned in the same breath as Bill Gates and she didn't have to invest a dime of her own money. This could have never happened in the old economic system."

Dressed in her signature business suits, and with her famous blonde coif as rigidly in place as her admirable business convictions, Whitman swept into the spotlight. From day one she has used her expertise in brand building to make eBay as well known to the public as McDonald's and Ford. More importantly, unlike her online rival at Amazon.com Jeff Bezos, Whitman has earned kudos for being able to show a profit.

"She doesn't tell investors that things will be profitable in three or four years," says an eBay executive. "She believes that now is the time. That's her motto. That's why since she's arrived eBay's popularity has

111

increased a thousand percent. Meg knows how to do business online as well as anybody out there."

Meg Whitman never planned on an Internet career. She grew up in Boston in a middle class home. Her best memories are of summer vacations, when her mother used to pile Meg and her older sister and brother into a beat up Ford Econoline van and drive coast to coast or up the Alaskan highway.

"We camped for three months. No hotels," she recalls. Whitman's mother Margaret was more of an adventurer, a refreshing throwback to the sixties peace and love generation.

In 1973, when Whitman was in high school, her mother traveled to China with actress Shirley MacLaine on a "spiritual journey". Margaret Whitman was the Boston housewife featured along with a group of "ordinary" American women in MacLaine's documentary "The Other Half of the Sky: A China Memoir". For young Meg it was an experience that would become ingrained in her mind. Her mother's experience in China with MacLaine brought enlightenment to the entire

Whtiman household. "Before the China trip, my mother told my sister to get a teaching degree - in case her husband couldn't support her," Whitman recalled. "When she came back from China, her perspective on women had changed completely. She told me, 'Go figure out what you want to do, and do it.'"

From that day Whitman knew her destiny. She wanted to become successful and rich as a businesswoman. After a summer selling advertising for her college magazine at Princeton University, Whitman bailed out of pre-med studies and switched to economics. She earned her undergraduate degree in 1977 and got her MBA from Harvard Business School two years later. It was at Harvard where Whitman made connections that became instrumental in her success later. Because she was an excellent student, headhunters were on her trail months before she graduated. After consulting with one of her professors she decided to take a position at Procter & Gamble before relocating to San Francisco in 1981 with her husband, Griffith R. Harsh IV, who received a residency in neurosurgery at the University of California at San Francisco.

In San Francisco, Whitman found lots of opportunity. She became in high demand. She worked for the Walt Disney Company from 1989-1992, working her way up to Senior Vice President of Marketing. At Disney she was credited for closing the deal on several major acquisitions, including the purchase of Discover Magazine.

"Meg was so talented and bright that everybody at Disney knew it would be only a matter of time before she would be snatched away," says former Disney marketing executive Bruce Sinclair. "Disney was a great stepping stone for her. It allowed her to network with some of the world's big honchos and it also increased her solid credibility."

After mulling over several lucrative job offers she joined the consulting firm Bain & Co., where she worked for eight years. In 1992 Whitman's family moved back to the east coast when her husband became director of the brain tumor program at Massachusetts General Hospital.

Her next job was with Florists' Transworld Delivery in Michigan in 1995. It was the one job Whitman still regrets taking. She had been hired by FTD, the florist-owned member association, to complete its transfer to a privately held company. But it didn't go smoothly. Several key FTD members campaigned vigorously against the idea and stiff competition cut FTD's market share significantly. Realizing that she had reached a dead end Whitman resigned from FTD in 1997. She worked briefly at Hasbro before moving to eBay.

Whitman's tenure at eBay has not always been a smooth one. In only her first day on the job, Whitman got a crash course on technical glitches when eBay's site crashed, bringing online trading to a standstill for more than eight hours. Keeping the site up became a top priority. Whitman put together a task force to study the technical problems of the site. After the team had reported back on what had gone wrong, discovering numerous networking flaws, Whitman made sure eBay added enough backup software and computer servers to make sure the site wouldn't crash.

115

"Meg was concerned about the site getting blocked off for hours at a time," said Silicon Valley technician Sol Luger. "She realized that pumping lots of bucks into fixing the problems was worth way more than having millions of dollars of trading lost because customers weren't able to access the site."

Despite Whitman's valiant attempts some major technical problems still persist. In January 1999, eBay experienced numerous short outages lasting between 10-15 minutes. Whitman called her old friend Scott McNealy (CEO of Sun Microsystems) and asked him for help. McNealy placed Sun technicians on call round the clock, seven days a week. Some shutdowns still happen but Whitman concedes that "it's bound to happen because the Internet's still in the developmental stages. This won't happen in a few years."

There's no doubt that the biggest headache for Whitman and eBay has been the sale of fake or fraudulent merchandise. The world's largest online auction has long been the target of such practices by scam artists and pranksters. You name it, its been sold on eBay, including human kidneys and illegal drugs. In several cases the pranksters have been caught and brought up on criminal charges. But eBay has been heavily criticized in the media for refusing to take the blame. In April 2000 a group of victims who purchased fake sports memorabilia on eBay filed a lawsuit seeking damages under California state law which prohibits the sale of such items. The suit raised the question of whether eBay should be held liable for the online deals that take place between buyers and sellers.

"The lawsuit could set a legal precedent for online auction sites," says Internet lawyer Robert Sheehan. "The biggest problem doing business on the web so far has been that the legal parameters are too vague. Sites like eBay refuse to be held accountable for dirty deals. It's not fair. If you buy something from a regular store and it turns out to be fake you can sue the pants off them. For some reason it's different online. Once people wake up and realize what's going on it will all change very quickly."

Ebay's response to the lawsuit was that it is not an auctioneer, as it does not hold merchandise, does not examine it and does not deliver it to buyers. Ebay describes itself as a "personal trading community", much like a classified ad. "I'm not sure how valid that argument is," Sheehan says. "Because then you can have anybody advertising goods on the net and make tons of cash, regardless of the product's authenticity. It becomes very dangerous territory."

In less than three years, Whitman has turned eBay upside down. She has increased the company's customer base from 750,000 to more than 12 million. She has also helped consumers buy their products via the oldest method of purchasing - bargaining. Her concept was adopted by every kind of selling on the Internet, including airplane tickets and flowers. Her new mission is to add larger and more expensive items such as antique cars to eBay's stock. And she's launched international auctions in Britain and Germany and is targeting several other countries. She also plans on setting up regional auction in

50 U.S. metropolitain areas to accommodate the larger items that people can't put in the mailbox.

And she has done everything to eat up the competition. In April 1999, Whitman announced that eBay bought the Butterfield & Butterfield Auctioneers Corporation, San Francisco's largest auction house, for $260 million in stock. Butterfield, founded in 1865, is the third largest auction house in the world after Sotheby's and Christies. It's known for dealing moderately priced art, collectibles and furniture. It also dealt in numerous high-profile auctions of items belonging to the rich and famous, including O.J. Simpson's Heisman Trophy. Whitman said the acquisition was made to expand eBay's catologue. "What eBay did for garage sales and collectibles we now want to do for higher end items," Whitman said. "We can grow the market and make it a lot more efficient."

Whitman didn't stop there. In June 2000 eBay bought Half.com, the site that allows buyer and sellers to trade items for fixed prices, for nearly $375 million in stock. Half.com's membership was about 250,000 when the deal was made. Since its founding in 1999, Half.com sold more than four million CDs, videos, movies and books at fixed prices listed by the sellers that are not allowed to exceed half of the original price.

"We have thought for some time that to have a truly global trading platform we needed to add the fixed-price format," Whitman said. "Even in this environment, great companies are hard to come by. Half.com had other suitors, and they had the opportunity to get more round of VC funding. They had gross margins and operating margins that were consistent with eBay's business model."

Whitman's maneuvering has created shockwaves throughout the high-tech industry. She has become the envy and role model of CEOs throughout the world. "When she's done she'll definitely be remembered as the pioneer of online auctions," says Internet stockbroker Cal Wiley. "She doesn't rest on past laurels. She keeps revolutionizing what she's already accomplished. There's not on CEO alive who wouldn't like to be in her position. By the time she decides to step down she could be the richest woman on the planet." Meanwhile, Whitman's long line of critics have been silenced. In fact, it seems that the only people who criticize her today are the people waiting in line to do business with her. Eventually she'll get to them and they'll get their chance. But only when she feels the time is right!

8

S*teven* B*allmer*

Years after a newspaper reporter misspelled his name as "Bullmer", in an article about an early version of Microsoft's Windows operating system, Steve Ballmer poked fun at the error at a trade show speech celebrating Windows. He joked that it was just one additional bug in a troubled product the company was committed to improving.

Bill Gates gets all the glory, but since taking over as Microsoft CEO in January 2000 Steven Ballmer certainly has made his mark. Gates stunned the world when he announced that he was promoting his longtime friend and company president, Ballmer, as chief executive officer of the powerful software giant Gates co-founded in 1975 with Paul Allen. Gates said the reason he stepped down was so he could concentrate his efforts more on the technical side in the future.

Although he describes 1999 as "being the worst year of my life", Gates denied that the move was made because of the antitrust suit against Microsoft which could result in the company's breakup. Ballmer was adamant that he was promoted because "we've been on a trajectory of this kind...for several months. We've been talking about making this final step and this just seemed like an appropriate time."

The day Ballmer replaced Gates experts cringed that Microsoft's stock would plummet. Investors, however, sent Microsoft's stock higher that day, apparently very comfortable with Gates's decision.

"Many people on Wall Street were shitting bricks when the decision was announced," says Wall Street broker Gary Klein. "But Microsoft prepared their investors properly. And the consensus unanimous. With Ballmer Microsoft was still a good investment."

Most experts, however, were convinced otherwise. "The biggest issue facing Microsoft today is whether to accept an AT&T-type settlement that involves breaking the company up or to continue the present litigation," Jamie Love told reporters. Love is the director of the Consumer Project on Technology, a Ralph Nader organization. "Many people think that the barrier to a breakup is more personal than financial. One interpretation of the announcement is that Bill Gates is further disengaging from the business, making it easier to consider a breakup of the company."

Gates had long been criticized by the media for being too narrow minded. Apple boss Steve Jobs once suggested that Gates's biggest problem was that he lacked culture.

"He'd be a broader guy if he had dropped acid or gone off to an ashram when he was younger," Jobs said.

Many felt that Ballmer's comical and offbeat personality would bring Microsoft a much needed breath of fresh air. "Everybody was tired of dealing with Bill Gates and his premeditated lines," says Internet columnist

Jan Jupiter. "Steve Ballmer has more personality. He provided spontaneity. He gives the media lines that make good copy. He's much more exciting to cover. Everything with Bill Gates was too well orchestrated."

Gates received Microsoft's new title of "chief software architect", which allows him to spend more time developing new software products and services. Microsoft had made Gates the world's richest individual, accumulating a fortune at more than $80 billion. If you haven't been on the planet earth for a while, Microsoft is the heavyweight champion of the software industry, with its Windows operating system on more than 90 percent of all personal computers.

The outspoken Ballmer was clearly hired at least to dispel rumors that a Microsoft breakup would be positive. In only his first day as CEO Ballmer said a breakup would be "absolutely reckless and irresponsible and the single greatest disservice that anybody could do to consumers in this country."

Anybody who knows Ballmer agreed that one thing that would not change at Microsoft was the company's aggressive nature. In fact, Ballmer had become known throughout the high-tech industry as the "Embalmer".

"Nobody who knows Steve well was concerned that Microsoft might suffer," says journalist Al Wilson. "Steve's one of the industry's sharpest shooters. It's almost impossible to pull the wool over his eye. He catches everything. He's the type of person that makes everybody's knees shake when he walks in a room."

Ballmer was raised in Farmington Hills, Michigan, a city near Detroit, which also produced legendary computer moguls Bill Joy and Scott McNealy, both of Microsoft's longtime archrival Sun Microsystems. Ballmer and McNealy remain close friends, and often consult with each other on major business transactions. They have been known to still occasionally room together at out of town industry functions.

"They've been close friends for years," says a friend of Ballmer's. "They email each other all the time and are always trying to get the upper hand when it come to business. It's all good fun and when they both

127

eventually retire they'll probably be golfing partners. Unlike many other people in this business they haven't let business interfere with their friendship."

Ballmer's father, an executive at Ford, preached to him the corporate loyalty that Ballmer has become renowned for at Microsoft. Ballmer is the butt of many jokes at Microsoft for refusing to drive a non-Detroit car. Today he drives a red Lincoln Continental. He even raised a fuss about appearing with Bill Gates in a Volkswagon for a company commercial in 1997. In the commercial, Gates and Ballmer were driving leisurely when they spotted a Sun computer abandoned on a curb. They picked up the computer and put it in the back seat but soon noticed a terrible smell. The final shot showed the computer in a trash can alongside the road. The commercial was shot shortly after McNealy referred to the Microsoft duo as "Ballmer and Butthead" during a speech.

"It was their way of getting back at McNealy in a fun way," said Josh Morgan, an engineer who has crossed paths with both Ballmer and McNealy over the years. "It became Microsoft's most popular commercial ever. And most of all it poked fun at the rivalry that underlines the PC industry. When McNealy saw it he wasn't too happy but still he couldn't help but laugh at it."

Ballmer's relationship with Gates goes back more than 25 years, when the two were classmates at Harvard in 1974. They met at Harvard's Currier House in Gates's sophomore year. They were close friends and often went to movies and parties together. The first time they went out together was to a double bill showing "Singin' in the Rain" and "A Clockwork Orange", Stanley Kubrick's futuristic film that played off "Singin' in the Rain's" theme song in a sinister blend of rape and violence. Back at Currier, Ballmer and Gates imitated the tune and got flack for it from a dorm mate who was deeply offended. In later years the duo often sang together at industry functions and parties.

"They both liked singing even though their talent was less than melodious.," says Chris Drake, the former Microsoft business consultant. "People love when they get up on stage together. It makes everyone in the room feel more comfortable. It can be extremely intimidating to sit in the same room with the two richest people on the planet."

At Harvard, unlike the introverted Gates, Ballmer was a big man on campus. The first day he arrived on campus Ballmer memorized the names and faces of his classmates from the class registry. It brought him instant popularity. He served as editor of the literary magazine, ad manager of Harvard's student newspaper "The Crimson" and was a leader of the "Fox Club", the all male frat like club where he inducted Gates to a bizarre ritual of drinking and storytelling.

Ballmer gets a kick out reminiscing about how he fared higher than Gates in math and economic tests. Ballmer says that the pair were "math nerds" who were stood out among the top students. Gates dropped out of Harvard to start Microsoft with his childhood friend Paul Allen. Unlike Gates, Ballmer graduated in applied mathematics. He visited Gates at Microsoft's headquarters of the time in Albuquerque, New Mexico, before taking a job at Procter & Gamble marketing cake mixes. In the spring of 1979 Ballmer decided to pursue his lifelong dream of making money in Hollywood. Ever since he was a kid Ballmer dreamt of being an actor. His heroes were Marlon Brando and James Stewart. On a whim, he convinced himself to take a shot at the movies. But he quickly realized that succeeding in Hollywood was more difficult that racking up high grades at Harvard. The closest he got to the big screen was parking cars and reading scripts.

In 1980 Gates convinced his old friend to stop studying at Stanford and to help him start up the then struggling new software company Microsoft. Ballmer signed on for $50,000 a year and became Microsoft employee number 28. Although his salary was relatively low, Ballmer received almost 10 percent of Microsoft as a signing bonus. The move paid off splendidly when Microsoft went public in 1986. Three years later, it also opened the door for Ballmer to buy nearly 1 million shares of Microsoft stock after a market correction. That deal today is worth several billion dollars.

In 1993 Ballmer became Microsoft's third billionaire after Gates and Paul Allen. "Gates hired Ballmer because he was the missing piece of the Microsoft puzzle," says a former Microsoft adviser, Glenn Baxter. "Gates and the rest of the initial Microsoft team were more concerned about the technical side of things. Ballmer is a natural salesman. He brought a business background to the company that was sorely needed. For years Ballmer did a magnificent job as the company's head of sales and marketing. Without his shrewd business sense Microsoft might have been doomed. Ballmer has made many of the big deals over the years that put Microsoft at the top of the business world."

During his 20 years at Microsoft one of Ballmer's chief missions was to manage the company's relationship with IBM. IBM was the client that Ballmer had to suck up to in order to succeed. "He did everything right to make the relationship solid," says former IBM employee Dan Baldwin. "He schmoozed with all the right people.

Everybody at IBM looked up to Steve. He had won their trust."

Ballmer's relationship with Gates has not been always strewn with roses. Over the years, the two friends have had some major falling outs. One time was in the spring of 1985, when Microsoft's deadline to produce Windows fell deeply behind schedule. Gates blamed Ballmer for the delay and threatened to fire him if Windows wasn't in the stores by the end of the year.

"I think Bill was just talking in the heat of the moment," said one Microsoft executive. "He would never fire Steve. He cherishes his friendship with Steve. Sure they've had their share of disagreements but its normal in any close relationship. They respect each other as much as any two human beings on earth. They truly love each other."

Gates truly showed how much he cherishes Ballmer when he asked him to be best man at his lavish, seaside wedding to Melinda French in 1994. In July 1998 Gates appointed him president to take responsibility for a "holy war" to increase customer satisfaction. "Steve brings a sense of stability to the company," says a Microsoft executive. "Although he's loud and likes to have a good laugh he's much more level headed than Gates. He knows how to deal with situations without flying off the cuff. He doesn't react on intuition or emotion."

It seems that somebody is always lecturing Ballmer on why he can't do something he has just finished doing. His motto is never be afraid to do the impossible. For example, as the media had already decided that Microsoft would be forced to split up long before the court's ruling, Ballmer refused to concede. He insisted that in the end Microsoft would have the last laugh. He told employees not to panic. In an April 2000 memorandum to his employees Ballmer said that business would continue as usual. "This company, which has done so many great things for consumers and for the American economy over the last 25 years, will not be broken up," Ballmer said. "No matter what the newspaper headlines say, absolutely nothing in the current case justifies breaking us up...I am extremely bullish about Microsoft's future. Microsoft

134

was born a competitor and we will continue to compete as we always have - fairly and vigorously...as we say in our ads 'the best is yet to come'".

The media was critical. Ballmer's goodwill gesture became perceived as an act of desperation. "Everyone at Microsoft was panicking," says business journalist Milton Cohen. "People started fearing for their jobs. Ballmer had to do something to restore calm. With his big background in public relations, he decided that sending a memo would turn things around. Instead it seemed to backfire. The employees were not used to receiving such a memo. They knew that something was up. Many employees started to update their resumes. The future looked very uncertain."

Ballmer had a five percent share of Microsoft worth almost $29 billion when he succeeded Gates as CEO. He was given more incentive when he became CEO. His Microsoft shares now total 239,626,854. Analysts say that his reputation as one of the industry's most ruthless negotiators will save Microsoft from splitting up. "He knows how to make a deal as well as anybody out there," says financial analyst Steve Fried. "When push comes to shove he'll save the day. He'll cut a deal with the Justice Department and everybody will go home happy. That's why Gates brought him in. He needed Ballmer to do his dirty work."

When he's not dealing with the company's plethora of legal problems Ballmer finds the time to take care of business. During his first years as CEO analysts forecasted Microsoft's consumer business would grow nearly 40 percent to more than $3 billion in revenue. Losses were expected to be $300 million, well below an estimated $500 million in 1998.

"This is all a result of Ballmer's leadership," said investment analyst Trey Ferguson. "He's a shrewd businessman who has a track record of making the books balance. The future looks brighter with Ballmer than it even did with Gates. Of course only time will tell, but if early indications are a sign of things to come Microsoft's future looks incredible, regardless of whether or not its broken up into two."

In June 2000, just days after Microsoft received Judge Thomas Penfield Jackson's ruling to split Microsoft in two and impose sweeping restrictions on its business practices, Ballmer called a press conference to unveil plans to transform Microsoft from a desktop leader to an Internet software company. The "Dot-Net" plan, Ballmer said, is essential for Microsoft's survival. If Microsoft doesn't produce software for the non-Windows world, Ballmer said, it will suffer irreparably in the new Internet-economy. "Dot-Net", scheduled for release in 2002, will produce a Web-enabled version of its Microsoft application suite. Customers would have the option to access it online for a monthly fee instead of having to buy a hard copy of Office software.

"Ballmer's a marketing genius," said journalist Harry Bukowski. "At a time when Microsoft was receiving non-stop negative press he turns the whole thing around into something positive. It would have been easy for him to just try to lay low and hope things would just die down. But instead he works diligently to put a positive spin on Microsoft. And it worked. More people were talking about Microsoft's "Dot-Net" plan that week than about the court ruling against them. Once again Ballmer was able to turn things around in his favor."

Judge Jackson's ruling on June 7, 2000 adopted the U.S. government's suggestion that Microsoft be split into two companies for 10 years. One company would own the Windows operating systems and would be forced to abide by a stern code of conduct restrictions. The other company would own everything else, including the Internet Explorer Web browser and the Microsoft Office suite. Judge Jackson ordered that the list of conduct restrictions imposed on Microsoft take effect in 90 days. He gave Microsoft four months to come up with a thorough breakup plan. A week later the software giant's lawyers asked the U.S. Court of Appeals for the District of Columbia Circuit to put Judge Jackson's order on hold pending the outcome of the appeal.

The move cleared the way for Judge Jackson to send the appeal directly to the Supreme Court, as requested by the Justice Department. Microsoft maintains that it did not illegally tie its Internet Explorer Web browser to its Windows operating systems, which was the major case made against them.

The software giant insists that Jackson's ruling of illegal "attempted monopolization" and "monopoly maintenance" had no foundation, especially considering arch rival Netscape Communications was not restricted from distributing its Navigator Web browser. Despite's Ballmer's hard line that Microsoft will never be broken up, even his biggest admirers think that he might be fighting a losing battle.

"If he manages to get through this unscathed it will be a big miracle," says Ballmer's colleague Edward Barnett. "Ballmer's doing everything he can to get Microsoft out of this big mess but it's highly unlikely that even his genius will be able to save the company from being forced to split up. The odds are stacked heavily against him."

Until the appeal is played out, for Ballmer, it's business as usual. And he continues his grueling lifestyle. He combines his love of sport with his intense work schedule. Ballmer leaves the house at 6 a.m., for a 5 to 10 mile run, even when he's on the road. He's cut down his 100 hour week work schedules but still puts in at least 70. Like many other wealthy computer CEOs Ballmer lives a rather modest lifestyle with his wife and two sons. His colonial home near Microsoft's Redmond, Washington headquarters is worth half a million dollars, nowhere near the 2-3 million dollar price tag on some of the city's upscale properties. His wife Connie is a former Microsoft PR executive. Ballmer's favorite hobby is playing pickup basketball. He remains an avid Detroit Pistons fan and attends most Seattle SuperSonics home games. "I think if he had to do it all over he'd own an NBA franchise," said basketball sports writer Larry Graham. "It's his passion. If he'd have a choice between sitting in front of the best computer in the world or watching the Supersonics I think it wouldn't be a difficult decision. He'd choose the latter."

9

Louis V. Gerstner

The mood at IBM and on Wall Street was almost one of disbelief when Louis V. Gerstner Jr. took over the CEO duties on April Fool's Day in 1993. Most people felt that it was the latest in a series of bad business decisions by the International Business Machines Corporation that had sent the company's stock plummeting.

Although Gerstner had a reputation as being a hard nosed businessman, he had no experience running an IT company. His previous good track record in leadership roles at RJR Nabisco, American Express and McKinsey & Co. did not automatically make him qualified to run an

IT heavyweight that was losing billions of dollars. Many of IBM's longtime employees sneered when Gerstner was hired.

"It practically made a mockery of the company," said New York business analyst Daryn Holmes. "IBM became the laughing stock of the computer industry. They hired a man with no track record in the computer industry to run the company. Many people felt that was the beginning of the end for IBM."

Today, however, IBM seems to be having the last laugh. With Gerstner, the company's stock rose immensely from an all-time low in August 1993 and split for the first time since 1979. And Gerstner has led IBM into the Internet world with a tenacious campaign to be at the forefront. He maintains that his goal is to make IBM the E in E-commerce. That means that IBM no longer is reliant on selling hardware as the company's bread and butter. They sell expertise and service. Yes, IBM still makes lots of computers, but the increased popularity of the Internet has forced them to branch out.

"I was one of those skeptics who thought IBM was making a big mistake," Daryn Holmes admits. "Lou Gerstner has managed to do the unpredictable. He's turned the company upside down and has restructured the company's direction in order to keep up with the times. If IBM hired a computer savvy person instead of Gerstner the company might have gone bust. Things were so bad that experts predicted IBM would have to be sold. It took a person like Gerstner who wasn't afraid of change to make sure IBM rose to the top of the computer industry again."

Soon after he was appointed CEO Gerstner made the bold prediction that the future of business would be on the Internet. Many people at IBM laughed at him and thought he was steering the company in the wrong direction. Of course, those critics look all look like fools today. Gerstner predicted many years before anyone else the future of the high-tech world.

"Killer applications of the future will be bookmarked Web sites rather than downloadable code," he said. "Anywhere on the Web people go to get something done - whether it's to trade stocks, renew a driver's license or get a college dree - will qualify as a killer application. This shift will mean more than added convenience for consumers and businesses. Any company with a presence on the Internet will be in the business of providing the killer apps that today are largely the stock of software vendors...If one billion people are going to do online banking...banks have to change the way they work."

Gerstner is known to be a workaholic who strongly believes in getting out in the marketplace and selling his product. Since joining IBM, he has traveled the world attending conferences, giving lectures and meeting with buyers in order to take IBM out of the doldrums. A sign in his office quotes from a novel by his favorite author, John le Carre: "A desk is a dangerous place from which to view the world."

"Big Blue" as IBM is famously nicknamed was in constant turmoil before Gerstner arrived. Its trademark mainframe computers, its number one product for so long, was criticized heavily for being outdated and too

144

cumbersome to use. The company's conservative approach was not greeted warmly by the rest of the computer business and its costs were much higher than those of its new competitors. IBM's board became concerned and made the decision to search for a new leader to bail them out. The business world was stunned when Gerstner was appointed. Gerstner, the head of RJR Nabisco, a cookie man, barely had the knowledge to even turn on a computer.

But the cookie man turned out to be the computer industry's toughest cookie. Gerstner, whose solid build makes him look more like a retired wrestler than a CEO, immediately cuts costs at the $72 million computer giant by more than $7 billion. The company's net income rose rapidly and stock was up from $51 when Gerstner took office to over $100 within the first few years. "We're going for leadership now," Gerstner preached to his employees. "We want to set the pace."

Gerstner devised a plan to channel IBM's energy into two vital directions. The first was providing services for other corporations, restructuring their entire information systems and managing them more effectively. The second strategy was providing the hardware, from the smallest personal computer to the giant mainframes, to efficiently deliver data over the Internet. IBM's service business grew from almost zero when Gerstner arrived to more than $15 billion within a few years. It will eventually be Big Blue's biggest money maker.

Under Gerstner the working environment at IBM has changed. Back in the old days it would take weeks and sometimes months to make major decisions. Gerstner insists on making quick decisions and to live with them till the end. A typical IBM meeting today does not involve overhead projectors and long presentations like was so common in the pre-Gerstner era. Under Gerstner, an idea is heard, it is debated for a short period and then a vote is held. When the result is announced there's no looking back.

"Lou's very well versed on all issues," says one IBM executive. "He doesn't like to prolong the process. His motto is go forwards and take action. Most of the time his final decision turns into gold. And when it doesn't he doesn't mope and start second guessing himself. He goes full steam ahead to the next idea."

Raised in New York as the son of a beer distributor, Gerstner does not ease up his workload on weekends. He takes home piles of documents so that he can stay on top of things. Every Saturday he spends hours in his home library catching up on new proposals and ideas. He calls his colleagues with questions and concerns.

"At first not too many people were very enthusiastic about this method," an IBM marketing executive remarked. "But when results started coming in people started sitting by their phones on the weekend waiting for Lou's calls. One of the biggest reasons that IBM rebounded so quickly under Lou is because he stays on top of things more than anybody I've ever met. His knowledge is powerful and he uses it to make incredible deals for the company."

Gerstner's rise to the top was not easy. At each job he's ever taken he's always been greeted by a long line of skeptics who were not receptive to his direct and speedy way of conducting business. And he's also had to overcome his share of health problems. Some twenty years before he joined IBM Gerstner lost part of two fingers on his right hand cut off in a lawnmower accident. Legend has it that as the surgeon was operating on his hand an impatient Gerstner pressed the doctor to speed the process up because he had a business meeting the next day. A few years after joining IBM Gerstner was bedridden for only five days after major eye surgery on a detached retina. He spent most of the five days on the phone to colleagues doing business deals.

"If Lou was an athlete he'd be a coaches dream," says Tom Reed, the computer marketing executive who has worked closely with several of the Best CEOs. "He'd always play hurt no matter how hurt he was. That's how he is in business. When he's sick it's impossible to keep him out of the office. His whole life is business. It's what he loves doing. He doesn't do it just for the sake of making money. He does it because it's his passion."

A native of Mineola, New York, Gerstner's background before IBM was primarily in marketing and finance, although he did receive a bachelor's degree in engineering from Dartmouth College in 1963. After deciding that he wanted to devote his life to business, Gerstner went to Harvard and graduated with an MBA in 1965. Gerstner received dozens of offers from major renowned companies across the U.S. He joined the management consulting firm of McKinsey & Co., Inc., becoming the youngest director ever in the firm's history. One of Gerstner's biggest clients wooed him away from McKinsey by making him an offer too good to refuse. American Express offered him the position of chief executive of its biggest subsidiary, American Express Travel Related Services. The company had been losing out in its battle against Visa and MastCard. Gerstner quickly reshaped American Express by repositioning its green card, reviving its gold card and introducing a platinum card.

"Lou is the hardest worker you will ever meet," said Deborah Jackson, a former American Express customer representative. "There's not many people out there who can come in an turn a company upside down the way Lou does. He's worth every penny he makes. He's the type of guy who can rescue a company no matter how bad the situation is."

Rescuing IBM was exactly what Gerstner did. Between 1991 and 1993, IBM had lost $15.4 billion and sales of its number one mainframes product had dropped by more than half. More than 100,000 employees were laid off. The company was on the brink of collapse. When Gerstner arrived he couldn't believe the state of disarray at the company. He later said, "it just looked like it was going into a death spiral. I wasn't convinced it was solvable."

Seven years later, Gerstner is hailed as a genius. In 1997 he cut the red ribbon on IBM's new Z-shaped headquarters in Armonk, New York. Gone was the old 420,000-square-foot, 900 persons headquarters that Gerstner inherited when he joined IBM. Gerstner's office in the old building was in a cramped room at the end of a long, forbidding corridor of private offices. IBM's legendary former chairman Thomas J. Watson Jr., began an expensive tradition of contracting such world famous architects as Edward Larrabee Barnes and Eero Saarinen to design the company's buildings, including the granite skyscraper with its celebrated public atrium on Madison Avenue and 57th Street in Manhattan. Gerstner wasn't interested in winning any aesthetic competitions. He quickly sold off the Manhattan shrine and billions of dollars worth of other IBM-owned real state. He wanted IBM to be in a building that is comfortable for its employees to work in and that didn't allow them to hide in their cubicles twiddling their thumbs. An open space concept would keep everybody on their toes.

The new building broke the mold of the traditional buttoned-down office in favor of a more open workplace. Gerstner and the other executive team at IBM now occupy the center wing of the Z-shaped structure, with most of the 600 other employees working in expansive spaces without being blocked off by walls and doors. The 280,000-foot building creates an open atmosphere working environment so that everybody is easily accessible.

"This is a building for IBM and its customers," Gerstner said. "It's not a building for architects. I like to walk the floors. There is a sharing that happens in an open environment. Those are values that I felt were important to IBM."

To respect the new building's $75 million budget Gerstner scrapped plans for an underground parking lot and brought in much of the old furniture from the old building. But he didn't cut corners on the new headquarters' technology. A high-capacity network connects every work station at IBM's corporate network and the Internet runs at speeds higher than most other companies. The conference room features the latest multimedia toys, including DVD's, two giant television monitors a personal computer and audiocassette players. All can be controlled by a touch screen on the conference table. Gerstner said that he wanted everything to be built around the new focus of IBM, network computing.

Gerstner's makeover paid off. The internal feuding that had crippled IBM for so many years was over. The company was one big happy family. A 20-

year-veteran IBM programmer described the atmosphere as being very warm.

"It was the first time I can remember that people come to work and say hello to each other," he said. "Before they'd come to work and bitch all day. It was more like we were getting paid to be backstabbers than computer professionals. For the first time I could remember I actually looked forward going to work."

Gerstner did not make many major personnel changes when he arrived at IBM. He told the old guard that their jobs were safe as long as they were willing to adapt to the new system. What Gerstner did was to add new people to fill in the holes in areas he thought were lacking. One of his first moves was to hire Abby Kohnstamm, the first woman to serve as senior vice president of marketing at IBM. Gerstner knew Kohnstamm well from the days they worked together at American Express when Kohnstamm served as his executive assistant. Many heads turned at IBM, a traditional bastion of male executives, when Gerstner announced the appointment.

Gerstner raised a few eyebrows for having a woman administer more than $1 billion in advertising and marketing spending in a marketplace where less than 5 percent of the top positions at the Fortune 500 companies, ranging from executive vice president to chairman - are women. "It was a radical move," says Wall Street Investment analyst Merle Weintrubb. "Unfortunately there are not many women in positions that high. IBM was in dire straits when Gerstner hired Ms. Kohnstamm. Many felt that it was going to be the final nail in the company's coffin."

Today, Gerstner has no regrets. He says that no matter what happens he tries to never look back. Meanwhile, Kohnstamm has become one of the biggest players in the advertising world. Kohnstamm completely changed the public's perception of IBM as yesterday's news. To do that she ceased IBM's working relationships with more than 80 advertising agencies around the world and hired Ogilvy & Mather Worldwide to handle the company's entire advertising campaign. Kohnstamm was old friends with Ogilvy's chief executive Shelly Lazarus, who promised to relaunch IBM with one voice and one direction around the world. Kohnstamm has since received many international marketing awards and is considered to be the key behind Gerstner's success.

"The old saying about CEOs is that they're only as good as the people they hire," says Merle Weintrubb. "Gerstner was a seasoned veteran when he joined IBM and he was well aware of this. So he brought in people he respected and had confidence in to work with him. His support team is rock solid. There's no monkey business going on, unlike the old days at IBM when it was known for being a free for all."

Some of the new marketing strategies Gerstner and Kohnstamm have introduced at IBM include a $600 million "e-business" campaign featuring customers of all kinds, from tattooed body-pierced Web designers to corporate execs in business suits. Its marketing slogan became that putting up a Web site was just the start of doing business in the new world economy, the Internet.

Gerstner signed up some of the biggest companies, including United Parcel Service, Charles Schwab and

155

Ford, to have IBM teach them how to use the Internet to boost their businesses. IBM also reached out to tens of thousands of small companies to help them get online. It runs their sites for a fixed cost which could run up to $200 a month. By 2001, IBM projects to have more than two million small-business customers.

"In the past IBM preferred doing business with the big boys and ignoring everyone else," Merle Weintrubb says. "Gerstner is good at math. The potential he saw by reaching out to the small guys was enormous. The numbers were so appealing that he's hired thousands of people just to chase business from small companies."

In an article he wrote for Business Week, Gerstner insisted that e-business is the present and future but warned against jumping onto the online bandwagon without exploring if it's worth it from a long-term, strategic standpoint. Many big companies have ignored Gerstner's advice, including Wal-Mart who started Walmart.com as a separate company. A March 200 study released by PricewaterhouseCoopers and The Conference Board said a piddling 28 percent of megacorps conduct online transactions through their sites and more than 80 percent of them receive 5 percent or less of their revenue from the Internet.

"It's not wise to do anything in life without carefully thinking it out and having the right knowledge," Merle Weintrubb says. "Wal-Mart's online site has had its share of problems. Companies thinking about venturing online should not ignore the advice of industry experts like Gerstner."

In November 1997 Gerstner received a vote of confidence from IBM's executive board. He received options for 2 million shares of stock for agreeing to stay on until he turns 60 years old in March 2002. The new stock options nearly equaled the 2.4 million Gerstner got when he first joined IBM in 1993. In an interview in the Wall Street Journal Gerstner said he decided to stay on because IBM was still in the neophyte stages of its resurrection. "The first phase was to get from survival to strength," Gerstner said. "And now we need to go from strength to leadership. I think that is going to take another five years."

In August 1999 Gerstner sold 400,000 of his shares for about close to $50 million. A few months earlier he sold an another 185,000 shares for close to $45 million. An aide to Gerstner said he has started to sell his shares regularly "as part of a regular program of tax planning and asset diversification which he began in 1998." In 1999, Gerstner cashed in $87.7 million in stock options. He earned a base salary and bonuses of $9.55 million. IBM's earning were a commendable $4.12 a share in 1999, up more than 25 percent from 1998. Financial experts predict a steady rise of growth at IBM of at least 13 percent over the next five years.

Some IBM shareholders are concerned that Gerstner might leave after September 2001, when his stock options are fully delivered. They're worried that there's not much reason for him to stay after that. Gerstner won't tip his hand. The man who once said "I'm not very comfortable in chitchat" will keep everybody hanging on the edge of their seats till the very end. But in the meantime, it's business as usual for him at "Big Blue".

"Lou will go down fighting till the very end," says Merle Weintrubb. "I'm sure he's already has planned how he wants to spend the rest of his life. But there's no reason to let everyone know his decision. It would take away precious time from doing business."

10

Lawrence Ellison

Larry Ellison might easily be the most loathed person in the high-tech business. His tantrums are extraordinary and his ego is even bigger. He's certainly not out to win any popularity contests. His trash talk about Bill Gates is legendary. He's also renowned for boasting about how many women he dates - often several a week. His passion for sailing and flying have turned him into high-tech's undisputed playboy. He rarely arrives at work before 10:00 a.m. He's seen so irregularly around Oracle that is own employees nicknamed him Elvis. His designer stubble and stylish Brioni suits landed him in the pages of Playboy magazine. He seems to get more attention for his outlandish antics than the products that put him there. If his life was a movie not even the most demented Hollywood scriptwriter could have conceived the story Ellison has so divinely crafted.

The most recent bizarre episode at Larryland, as Oracle's Redwood Shores, California campus is aptly called, was in late June 2000 when it was revealed that Ellison hired a prominent Washington detective firm to investigate groups sympathetic to its archrival Microsoft. Ellison's detectives found a plethora of document embarrassing to Microsoft in the midst of its antitrust battle with the government. Ellison was blasted in the media for what was generally perceived to be very unethical and bordering illicit practices.

"When it was revealed that Ellison hired detectives it became clear that he's become so big, at least in his own mind, that now he thinks he can take the law into his own hands," said business journalist Walter Scanlon. "He has no respect for the authorities or for people's privacy. Who the hell does he think he is? He should mind his own business and let the proper people carry out their investigations. I clearly see his efforts as an attempt to interfere with the law."

Ellison adamantly points out that there was nothing wrong with hiring detectives. "Some of the things our investigator did may have been unsavory," Ellison said. "Certainly from a personal-hygiene point they were. I mean, garbage - yuck." Ellison insisted he did nothing unethical or illegal. In fact, he says, his PI's found sufficient evidence that Microsoft was surreptitiously funding "front groups" in order to sway public opinion in its favor. Ellison said that as a concerned citizen he felt it was his job to perform a "civic duty". He referred to Bill Gates as a "convicted monopolist".

"Ellison has no respect for anyone but himself and his lame excuses just go to show that he's trying to weasel his way out of another stupid move he made," said former Wall Street Journal contributor Alan Feldman. "He should be held accountable for his actions. It's not up to him to try to resurrect Watergate. Whatever he does against Bill Gates and Microsoft is a big conflict of interest. He's said forever that he'll do anything to put

Oracle ahead of Microsoft. He clearly has shown that and it's getting a bit ugly."

Ellison's spying on the enemy tactics left his foes at Microsoft angry and out for revenge. "They've set new standards for hypocrisy and disingenuousness, even for Microsoft," said Microsoft spokesperson Mark Murray. Many people who Ellison targeted said that the PI's tactics were extremely unethical. The Association for Competitive Technology accused Ellison's spies of trying to buy its garbage. Other organizations accused the investigators of stealing laptops from their offices that had information in them relating to Microsoft. Meanwhile, Ellison's army of longtime critics in Silicon Valley were having the biggest laugh. "Larry Watching" has become a popular sport over the years in Northern California.

"I'm sure it's not the first time Ellison's done something like this," said Terry Collins, a San Jose computer analyst. "It's people like him who give our industry a bad name. I hope he feels really low now. Nobody will ever trust him again. He's done so many things over the years at other people's expense to further his own career. Half the time he makes up white lies. I don't think there's anybody I've ever had as much disrespect for."

Ellison insists he didn't do anything wrong. He said he had no idea that the investigators would sift through garbage. He refused to offer any apology.

"What exactly did we do?" he said. "What is our corporate espionage? Our corporate espionage is to find out that Microsoft has hired all these companies, these front organizations, and while they pretend to be independent, publishing all sorts of things that are anti-Oracle and pro-Microsoft."

The "Dumpster" incident, as it was dubbed by the media, took an immediate heavy toll on Oracle. Only days after Oracle's mercurial president and chief operating officer Ray Lane resigned. Speculation was rife that Lane resigned because he disapproved of "Dumpster". Another story had it that while Lane, 53, was on vacation with his two daughters in Oregon Ellison called him and relieved him from most of his key duties and signing authority without much explanation. Lane refused to confirm what the actual reasons were for his departure. But he did admit that he disagreed with the direction in which Ellison was steering Oracle. And privately, he told close friends that he had had enough of Ellison's outlandish tactics.

"I just didn't fit," Lane said. "I've never seen a CEO micromanage every decision at a company. It's strange."

According to one Oracle insider Lane grew tired of putting up with his flamboyant boss. He disapproved of Ellison's lifestyle and spending habits and also the inconsistency in his behavior. "Larry reneged on several promises he had made to Ray," the employee said. "Larry had a vision which was completely different from Ray's. They couldn't find a common ground. In the end the spying incident might have been the last straw for Ray."

Marc Benioff, the former Oracle executive who left in 1999 to startup Salesforce.com, was not surprised that Ellison and Lane didn't see eye-to-eye. Benioff, who remained close friends with Ellison, appointed him to his new company's board of directors until he found out that Ellison started developing products that compete with his company.

"Larry is a very aggressive guy and if he thinks Oracle's at risk and not as strong, he makes a change," Benioff said. "Larry is trying to plan Oracle's future around taking its software and making it online services. Ray's skills are much more that he's a strong relationship builder and strong at running a sales and consulting force."

Ellison's rivalry with Gates has been frought with irony and contradiction. It stems back to when they both started software companies in 1977. And they both became the world's richest men. But the similarities stop there. Thrice divorced, Ellison is renowned for living in life's fast lane. He's a renowned playboy and he once tried to buy a $20 million Russian MiG. Gates's motivation is in sharp contrast.

"There's no comparison between the two," says entertainment author Esmond Choueke. "Gates is more serious about being an innovator. Ellison is more concerned about lining his pockets so he can wine and dine pretty young blondes. In one hundred years everybody will remember Bill Gates. I don't think many will know the name Larry Ellison."

On April 28, 2000, Ellison finally surged ahead of Gates in terms of wealth. Although his celebration didn't last long - a couple of months later Gates was No. 1 again in Fortune 500 - he finally accomplished what he wanted to do for so many years. He dethroned Gates as the world's richest person. Ellison's worth was listed as $53 billion, compared to Gates's $51.75 billion. Ellison's 663 million shares of Oracle closed that day at $79.94, compared to Gates's 742 million Microsoft shares at $69.75. The new ranking was a far cry from a Forbes lists six months prior, when Gates was listed on top at $85 billion. Ellison trailed badly at $13 billion. Many experts felt that Microsoft's antitrust battle was the reason Gates fell to number two.

"Let's face it if Microsoft wasn't in midst of a major lawsuit there's no way Gates would be second," said Wall Street stock analyst Brian Frank. "Ellison was blowing his own bubble for no reason. He looked like a fool when he fell behind Gates again shortly after. He had been telling everyone that Gates was finished. No way. Ellison is so full of himself. He knew it wouldn't last. He never said the truth, that Gates was embroiled in a legal battle. He's so sneaky."

Several months before, Ellison told journalists at his mansion in the exclusive Pacific Heights area of San Francisco that Microsoft should be broken not into two, but three companies. Early in the long antitrust legal proceeding, Ellison called Gates the "PC pope" because of his company's monopoly over who is allowed to build PCs. A couple of years earlier Ellison was publicly lambasting Gates during a keynote address at Comdex in which he mocked a white paper by Gates that described a world where applications and data would one day be permanently on big computers. "We agree. We're in the megaserver business," Ellison said. "Bill's vision of the future is today's Internet. That's how the Internet works, Bill."

Unlike Ellison, Gates didn't take it personally. "He's way above that now," said Silicon Valley venture capitalist Aaron Diamond. "He feels the same way Warren Buffet did when Gates passed him seven years ago. He doesn't care. Bill's always said that the toughest thing when you get to the top is staying there. He knows better than anybody that it won't last forever."

The quintessential stories about Larry Ellison involves the pickup lines Ellison uses on women. Several women insist that Ellison promised them trips, cash and even a luxury car when he first asked them out. One 33-year-old former Oracle employee, who was fired shortly after an affair with Ellison, was awarded a $100,000 settlement from him. Ellison accused her of forging an email message to make it seem she was fired for refusing to adhere to Ellison's sexual demands. Ellison admitted to the affair and to making her and other women offers of $150,000 loans and $50,000 Acura sports cars. One year Ellison admits that he bought four Acura cars.

"He's an insatiable hustler when it comes to both business and women," says Ryan Armstrong, a former

Silicon Valley based journalist who has contributed to the New York Times. "Like most guys in his field he has an amazingly large ego. The only difference between Larry and the others is that he's not pretentious about it. He admits that he's a playboy and hustler. The other guys don't but let me tell you I know most of them personally and there are very few who aren't banging three or four other women on the side and their wives have no clue. CEOs like Larry Ellison think that they have a license to live without rules and ethics. But then again, if you or I had their power and wealth would we be different? I doubt it."

A woman who claims she had an affair with Ellison before he got married to his second wife, said that he was an incredible lover. The woman, who requested anonymity, describes Ellison as a "sex maniac". "He liked to have sex over and over," the woman said. "He's in great shape. He can last for hour and hours. We once made love in a hot tub for more than six hours. And he still wanted more. I got out of the tub because my skin was turning into a prune. One time he visited me the night before a major business meeting. He was supposed to spend the evening going over notes. Instead we drank champagne for several hours and then we made love till the wee hours of the morning. The next morning he went to the meeting totally unprepared. He said he was quite worried. Later that day he called me and told me it was one of the best meetings he ever had. He had raised a lot of money. If Larry gets laid he gets paid. That's what motivates his success."

Ellison's close friends accuse him of using women to camouflage his rough experiences growing up on the South Side of Chicago, a place Ellison calls "the oldest and worst black ghetto in the United States."

Born in 1944, just as the second world war was coming to an end, some of Ellison's childhood heroes included baseball greats Mickey Mantle and Sandy Koufax. Ellison was not popular during his public school days and often acted up in class to try to get the attention of his peers.

"He had the reputation for being the class clown," says Arnold Schwartz, who also grew up in what Ellison calls the "Jewish Ghetto". "The girls didn't like him that much then and he was a bit of a pain in the ass to his teachers. He wasn't extremely popular."

Ellison says that although he lived in a very rough neighborhood it was nothing like the ghettoes today. "The ghettoes of today and the lower middle-class neighborhoods of today are dominated by guns and drugs," Ellison recalled in an interview. "I didn't even know I lived in a bad neighborhood. I was unaware of it. No one told me. And I didn't discover it until I left."

Ellison, however, had a penchant for science and math. He always excelled in these areas and was told by his teachers that if he stopped clowning around that he would have a good shot at making something of himself in a field related to these subjects.

Ellison, like Bill Gates, eventually dropped out of college without a degree. He never took a computer science class in his life. He was completely self-taught. He says that he just picked up a book and started following its programming instructions. Then he used his own creativity to program unique things.

173

"I liked to experiment," Ellison said. "I wasn't afraid of failure. If something didn't work I went back to the drawing board."

Tired of Chicago, Ellison headed west to California's burgeoning high-tech scene. He landed a job at Amdahl, which was owned by Fujitsu of Japan. On a business trip to Japan he fell in love with Japanese culture, something which still sticks with him today.

"When I visited the City of Kyoto I was stunned," Ellison recalled in an interview for the Smithsonian Institute. "It was one of only two times in my life I was stunned. The first time was when I first saw Yosemite Valley. I simply didn't know such a thing could exist. Kyotos wasn't on the messianic scale of Yosemite Valley and other creations of God. It was interesting, because it was the same natural - if I can use the word design - but on a much smaller scale, on a much more human and intimate scale. Japanese culture is very interesting, and it has influenced me - and let me tell you - a great deal. The Japanese are at once the most aggressive culture on Earth and the most polite."

In 1977, with an investment of only $2000, Ellison shelled out $2000 of his own money to start Oracle. His story is the classic American rags to riches saga. He didn't receive any outside funding. In those days the words venture capitalists were non existent for software companies. They only invested in hardware companies. It took Ellison more than two years to get the first version of Oracle on the market. The first version was sold and installed in November, 1979. Ellison did the installation himself and also taught the training course.

Oracle was contracted for different projects with companies like Memorex, Tandem and Amdahl. Ellison built up Oracle's bank account by a couple of hundred thousand dollars doing consulting. Ellison says that the company was profitable from day one. "We never, ever lost money," he says. "In fact, the only time we lost money was one quarter. One quarter, unfortunately, I think, in fiscal year 1990 we lost money."

"You can criticize Larry Ellison all you want but you can't deny the hard work he put in to become so successful," says Wall Street stock analyst Jason Singer.

175

"Sure he's become the most flamboyant person in the business today. But I respect him for trying to reap some of the benefits of success. A lot of people accumulate wealth and don't know how to enjoy it. Not Larry, he lives every day like it's his last."

Ellison says the key to his success was not being afraid to take risks. "There is really nothing riskier than not taking risks," he said in the Smithsonian interview. "I often say that when you think you have this really great idea and everyone else thinks you're nuts, there's one or two possibilities. You have a really great idea; the other possibility is you're nuts. So, you know, we were told we were nuts when we tried to build a commercial version of a relational database. We were told we were nut when we tried to move our software to massively parallel computers. Whenever you're just doing the same thing everyone else is doing, the you can hope for is parity, you know, or small advantages, to do it 10 percent better or 20 percent better or even 30 percent better, but not a thousand times better."

Ellison often takes verbal risks, making outlandish predictions to attract publicity for Oracle. Early in the 1990s he turned heads when he predicted that the Web would rise up and turn the PC into a dinosaur. Nobody threw away their keyboards but he definitely has had the last laugh.

"He was considered a little over the edge," said analyst Charles E. Phillips of Morgan Stanley Dean Witter. "But that's how you get people's attention. He makes crazy predictions, and sometimes, they actually come true."

While the 6 foot tall playboy cavorts with society's elite, including Bill Clinton and Jack Kemp, he continues to constantly bask in the media spotlight for his unorthodox style. In January 2000, after almost two years fighting San Jose International Airport's curfew and nine violation citations, Ellison sued the city of San Jose for the right to take off and land all night long. In the suit Ellison accused the city of unfairly enforcing an ordinance that bans plans weighing more than 75,000 pounds (34,000 kg) from using the airport between 11:30

177

p.m. and 6:30 a.m. Ellison's Gulfstream V weighs about 90,500 pounds (41,000 kg) at take-off when fully fuelled. He claimed that his luxury jet is much quieter than most of the planes that weigh less.

"This curfew is intended to fight noise, but it is written on weight," Ellison told reporters. "I'm not saying that curfews are bad but they have got to be non-arbitrary and non-discriminatory." An official for the city of San Jose said that Ellison's suit was without foundation and would be thrown out of court.

"The man's a marketing genius," says journalist Daniel Klein. "Even if he loses he'll still get millions of dollars of free publicity. It definitely won't hurt Oracle."

During his ascension to the top it has not always been smooth sailing. In 1998, on the day after Christmas, Ellison was jolted awake. That day in Sydney, Australia, Ellison's maxi-yacht Sayonara managed to evade a torrential storm in the 630-mile Sydney-to-Hobart yacht race. Six of the 1,135 sailors in the 54th running of the yacht race were killed. Dozens of other crew members were injured, and 57 had to be lifted from damaged yachts, sinking rafts and the sea itself by helicopters and coast guard craft in the largest maritime civilian rescue operation in Autralia's history. Only 44 of the 115 boats that started the race managed to finish. Ellison's Sayonara yacht won the race in two days and 19 hours but Ellison was in no mood for a victory party. He looked visibly shaken and did everything he could to console the victims' families.

"The tragedy brought out the compassionate side in him, a side that not many who know him are used to seeing," said Australian boat writer Jarred Hughes. "I think that for the first time in his life Larry Ellison realized how fragile and sacred life really is and that no matter how much money you have it's not more powerful than life's natural disasters. His boat won the race but it really did seem insignificant to him. When he won in 1995 the scene was much different. The champagne flowed for days after. This time the celebration was one of mourning for the fatal victims. I'm sure he'll be back for future races but the 1998 horror will always loom large over him. I don't think he'll ever get over the tragedy that took the lives of his fellow competitors."

The plethora of dot-com companies that have fallen by the wayside in 2000 has not slowed down Ellison's lavish lifestyle one iota. He's spotted more than ever spending on new cars, $3,000 bottles of wine, and wild parties for his friends.

"Larry will only slow down when he dies," says a close friend of Ellison. "He enjoys life to the fullest and along the way he's been extremely generous to the people who surround him. People like to talk behind his back because they're jealous. But let me tell you, Larry has never hurt a fly. Sure he does crazy things sometimes but it's only because he wants to succeed. He wants to be the best. Can anybody criticize him for that? I don't think so."

While Ellison plans his next move and next wild party, some of which have been estimated to cost over half a million dollars, he monitors the stock market closely. He looks at every move his competitors are making and creates new strategies to stay on top. "The only way to win is to stay ahead," Ellison once said. "And to stay ahead you have to be on the ball, or else..."

Love him or hate him, the future for Larry Ellison looks good despite recent turmoil at the company's San Meteo offices. Oracles' fourth-quarter earning on June 20, 2000 showed that sales of its flagship database software were running out of steam. Ellison, however, insisted his company was in better shape than ever.

"The Internet has lowered our cost of doing business, broadened our distribution and marketing," he said. "It's unbelievable. I'm not conning you."

Epilogue
Dot-Com or Dot-Bomb?

It wasn't long ago that if you put a good idea down on paper your chances of securing several million dollars in start-up money from a venture capitalist seemed as easy as ordering take-out from a fast food restaurant. People were able to get rich quick! Today, however, the situation has changed dramatically. It seems that everybody from the venture capitalists to the general public has grown increasingly querulous about the future of the dot-com world. It has become an extremely tight-fisted market.

It seems like yesterday that every 22-year-old out of college had hopes of getting hired by a new start-up with the goal of becoming a millionaire before turning 25. Perhaps they still do. There's no denying, however, that things are a bit different.

All that changed remarkably in 2000 because of the low performance of the stock market. It is not as common anymore to see these young adults cashing in on their booming start-ups going public. Many high-tech workers are carrying the burden of worthless stock options.

During the first 11 months of 2000, almost 25,000 dot-com employees - the bulk being in Silicon Valley and San Francisco - were laid off, according to outplacement firm Challenger Gray & Christmas reports. Even more alarming was the fact that a record 209 initial public offerings were scrapped in the same period as a result of the shaky stock market. These statistics forced many workers to polish up their resumes and to invest more wisely.

Still, however, most financial analysts believe that the market will rebound and that people should not panic. Venture capitalists are more careful but they still keep an open mind.

"Times have been tough but those who didn't succeed have nobody to blame but themselves," said Jerry Mason, who works in New York for an Internet consulting firm whose clients include many highly successful dot-com companies. "Too many people tried to get rich too quick, without doing the necessary homework about how to run a business. You can't make it in any business that way. You've got to work hard and have a long-term plan. So many young kids have come into my office with an idea of an Internet company and the first question they ask is 'how can I raise $10 million to get started'.

"It's ridiculous. They don't realize that by getting venture capitalists involved that, essentially, they're giving up more than 80 percent of their business. They're more interested in bragging to their friends that they have millions in the bank, which really isn't their and when

185

they blow it all they'll have one big debt hanging over their shoulders forever."

The number of Internet dot-com's struggling today doesn't have many people believing that the Internet is a passing fad. More people are hooked up online than ever. Wireless companies seem to be the wave of the future while highly publicized ventures like Priceline.com are holding on by the skin of their teeth. Increased competition from other Internet travel sites and airlines themselves have taken away a lot of customers from Priceline's main business. And Priceline's attempt to expand into other markets has failed miserably.

In November 2000, Priceline's head of the Internet seller's auto-services business Maryann Keller resigned along with three other top executives. Keller, a highly respected auto-industry analyst who joined Priceline.com in July 1999, told The Wall Street Journal that she left because the company kept cutting back on employees. The final straw was when she was told to lay off half of her 23-person staff. Keller told the Journal she doesn't think selling cars online is part of the Internet's future.

"For car buying, the Internet is an idea whose time has not yet come and may never," she said.

The resignations seemed to be the least of Priceline's problems. In October 2000, WebHouse Club, an independent licensee of Priceline that took online bidding on gasoline and groceries, closed its doors. The same day Perfect Yardsale, which sold second hand goods through the Priceline Web site, also announced that it was shutting down.

"It's simply a case of taking on way more than you can chew," says a former longtime analyst at Citigroup, the No. 1 U.S. financial services company. "Before you walk you must learn to crawl. It's that simple. It's important not to be fooled by all the failures. It's an Internet revolution and in any revolution you have both winners and losers, and not much left in between. We've been hearing too much recently about the losers but let me tell you that everybody who is in the know will agree that the Internet is the future and that nothing can stop it. That's why it is so important for people to study how the winners became so successful and to follow their winning ways."

New York economics analyst Gene Law is not worried about the decline of the high-tech stocks. He points out that it wasn't too long ago in the late eighties that Silicon Valley was being dubbed the "Valley of Death", due to abysmal computer sales and a chip trade war with Japan that left thousands of high-tech workers jobless. Law predicts that this time the decline will be short-lived and that people should not fear another recession. He points out that there are over 7,000 high-tech firms in Silicion Valley alone today that are producing more than $100 billion a year in revenue. The rest of the world, Law says, is in a similar position. Unemployment is steadily decreasing because of new jobs being created in high-tech.

"People tend to exaggerate the situation," Law says. "They should look much closer at the big picture. People in high-tech are spending more money than ever. You don't see the Larry Ellison's of the world eating at cheap restaurants. The people who have fallen will rebound because there's more jobs than manpower. The Internet is alive and well. Until the market rebounds what you'll see is high-tech employees making wiser investments. They won't take big risks. They'll pour their cash into more conventional investments, like bonds, real estate and money-market funds. But I guarantee you that they won't be looking to switch professions. They know where the future of the world's economy lies. In their computer!"

The two Best CEOS:

Top: Bill Gates with Bill Clinton
Bottom: Apple's Steve Jobs

Who's Your Favorite CEO?

Take a deep breath, and think about who you would like to nominate for the next exciting edition of Best CEOs to be published in 2002.

Please send a letter of no more than 1000 words. Make sure to include the CEOs company, name and location.

All letters should be sent to:

Best CEOs - Volume 2

PO Box 23140

Ottawa, Ontario

K2A 4E2

Or email: bestceos@ogobooks.com

Amazon.com's Jeff Bezos shares a laugh with his fans.